Education Is Special for Everyone

Education Is Special for Everyone

How Schools Can Best Serve all Students

Janet D. Mulvey, Bruce S. Cooper,
Kathryn F. Accurso, and Karen Gagliardi

ROWMAN & LITTLEFIELD
Lanham • Boulder • New York • London

Published by Rowman & Littlefield
A wholly owned subsidiary of The Rowman & Littlefield Publishing Group, Inc.
4501 Forbes Boulevard, Suite 200, Lanham, Maryland 20706
www.rowman.com

16 Carlisle Street, London W1D 3BT, United Kingdom

British Library Cataloguing in Publication Information Available

Library of Congress Cataloging-in-Publication Data

Mulvey, Janet D.
Education is special for everyone : how schools can best serve all students / by Janet Mulvey, Bruce S. Cooper, Kathryn Accurso, and Karen Gagliardi.
p. cm.
Includes index.
ISBN 978-1-4758-0763-9 (cloth : alk. paper) — ISBN 978-1-4758-0764-6 (pbk. : alk. paper) — ISBN 978-1-4758-0765-3 (ebook)
1. Inclusive education—United States. I. Cooper, Bruce S. II. Accurso, Kathryn, 1953- III. Gagliardi, Karen. IV. Title.
LC1201.M85 2014
371.9'0460973—dc23
2014010633

Printed in the United States of America

Contents

Introduction

Overview of the Book: What Problems, What Solutions?

Special education advocates have worked to provide an equal opportunity for all students with special needs. Laws have been enacted that seek to protect children from bias related to their special needs and have sought to educate the public and gain their understanding and support. Children with disabilities are no longer relegated to separate facilities, institutions, or home schooling. They are diagnosed, evaluated, and—based on assessment finding—given specific strategies designed to help reach individual potential. And this has been good.

The questions being answered in this book are as follows:

1. What strategies are in place to motivate and engage the traditional student to prepare them for knowledge and skills for the twenty-first century?
2. To what extent have we overlooked the importance of challenging our students without disabilities?
3. How are we preparing future talent to move the United States forward economically, democratically, and socially?

Friend and Bursuck (1999) addressed the concern of inclusion, raised twenty-four years ago:

> There is no issue that causes more controversy in special education among teachers, administrators, and parents than inclusion. Inclusion represents the belief or philosophy that students with disabilities should be integrated into the general education classroom whether or not they can meet traditional curricular standards. (p. 4)

Laws and regulations enacted to provide opportunity for children with special needs are frequently misunderstood, often resulting in placements benefitting no one. Least restrictive environment (LRE), one of the mandates of the Individuals with Disabilities Education Act (IDEA), is perhaps among the most widely implemented and seriously misunderstood regulations, having a major impact on classrooms, teachers, and students.

The National Dissemination Center for Children with Disabilities (2010) defines the least restrictive environment (LRE) as follows: "In basic terms, LRE refers to the setting where a child with a disability can receive an appropriate education designed to meet his or her educational needs, alongside peers without disabilities to the maximum extent possible" (np).

Regulation 300.114(a) further states, "Special classes, separate schooling, or other removal of children with disabilities from the regular educational environment occurs only if the nature or the severity of the disability is such that education in regular classes with the use of supplementary aids or services cannot be achieved satisfactorily" (National Dissemination Center for Children with Disabilities, 2010).

THE THEME OF OUR BOOK

In this book, we investigate these five questions: (1) What is the least restrictive environment for average, above average, and potentially gifted students? (2) How are these students being served and affected by the emphasis on special education programs and policies today? (3) Where are the regulations to protect them from classrooms where most attention is paid to the student with special needs without the required supplementary aids or services? (4) What has happened to a free and appropriate education for students without disabilities? (5) How might major attention to the least able affect our society as we fall behind other nations?

In many cases, current inclusion trends have relegated the traditional student to the background—even ignoring them—while those with special needs are given more attention from the sole teacher in the classroom. These financial restraints have caused many schools and districts to place students with special needs into regular classrooms without the support and aids that were originally intended by the law. In some inner-city schools, up to 40 percent of students can have special education designations and one teacher in each classroom is responsible to show learning growth for each and every student.

Lower standards, less motivation and engagement, and higher dropout rates among poorer districts have been compounded from this inclusion policy. The courts, schools, and districts have it wrong, and the country is beginning—and will continue—to feel the consequences. The United States is already being affected, as the nation ranks lower on international comparative assessments. In fact, the Programme for International Student Assessment (PISA) ranks the United States below some third world countries, especially in literacy, math, and the sciences. Scoring seventeenth in literacy, the United States also scores below average on both math and science, according to the 2009 PISA results (Program for International Student Achievement, 2009).

The overall health of the United States is dependent on the proficiency of its populace; economic prosperity, industrial strength, military prowess, and a strong democratic government all hinge on the education of its people. Poor education; high school dropouts; and fewer postsecondary graduates from colleges, universities, and trade schools exact a huge economic toll on the United States.

America's colleges and universities still rank among the best in the world; thus, they attract students from all countries and nationalities. The problem: international students outperform domestic students, taking their knowledge and skills back to their respective countries, resulting in a strengthening of foreign infrastructures. Good for them—but what about us?

Debra W. Stewart, reports that student enrollments in American graduate programs have increased by 8 percent for international students but only by 1 percent for American students from 2002 to 2012, causing concern for the future of our well-educated domestic human capital. She indicates, "The U.S. Department of Labor has forecast a 22 percent rise in jobs requiring at least a master's degree from 2010 to 2020, and a 20 percent rise for jobs requiring doctorates" (quoted in Patton, 2013, np).

In particular, concern is increasing about the widening chasm between foreign and domestic enrollments in the sciences, math, and engineering. If our public elementary, middle, and high schools do not prepare and ready our students for higher education and learning, we will continue to be outdistanced and eventually lose our competitive status in international affairs.

This book examines the current status of the inclusion classroom and the expectations for teachers to teach students with special needs along with the average and above children. We research and report on issues of teacher preparation, placement for students with special needs, education law, and financial implications. Case studies are presented to illustrate the effects on our programs locally, nationally, and internationally. Each case illustrates conditions in public schools and districts in urban and suburban settings through the eyes of teachers, administrators, and postsecondary educators.

Attention is given to the current once-yearly test scores that determine competency and have often unraveled the true meaning of teaching and learning for our children now and into the future. Policies driving special education need to be examined and reformed to benefit all students and to awaken the spirit of educating the young for the future leadership and prosperity of our society and country.

SOLUTIONS, IF ANY

This book hopes to show educators and policy makers how to serve all children without ignoring any of them. How can we continue to help the less able, "disabled," and troubled kids while making sure that schools do not sacrifice the other pupils (e.g., gifted, talented, average, and regular education children)? Do we do this in one classroom with one teacher, in one classroom with a number of teachers and specialists, or by integrating flexible programs according to the strengths of the students? How do we change the programs that are clearly not working to help all students to a better education and a better life?

And so we, as educators, must recognize the problem and begin sensible solutions based on research without interference from politics. We should embrace the original intent of public schooling and have some common classes for everyone, to teach them about each other, while likewise offering special education for children with differing needs, backgrounds, languages, and abilities. How do we do this effectively, universally, and economically? All for education and education for all!

This book focuses on and analyzes what happens in the classroom to the regular, general education students—not to mention the gifted—in the widespread inclusionary classroom. Have we invested more resources in serving the special needs of the growing special education population, thus, sacrificing our more able students and our national and international rankings and productivity? When competing with other countries, the United States ranks, sadly, twenty-fourth in math and seventeenth in literacy (OECD, 2010).

The inclusion model (i.e., involving students with disabilities) has become the trend in our general education classrooms in the public school system. Teachers are responsible and expected to adapt curriculum, methods, and practices to meet the needs of these students—as mandated by law—while often neglecting the more able and brighter children.

This book presents the issue of equity for all, looking at who benefits and who is left behind in our current system. While much has been said and written about the needs, programs, and results of inclusion for students with disabilities, little to nothing has been done to examine the effects of these programs on the average and above average children.

This book focuses on the "others" in the classroom, the nonclassified, average, and above average students. This book will be of interest to parents; school administrators; members of school boards; and teachers; as well as federal, state, and local policymakers. Here, we address the diverse needs of all children, including those with special needs, as well as the average and above child.

In this book, we ask if our society is in effect sacrificing the education and achievement of our average and brighter students on the altar of inclusion. To this end, we examine current practices in public schools, including:

1. Placing students with special needs into the general education population;

2. The efficacy of the practice of teaching all students (with different needs and abilities) in one classroom;
3. The effects on the achievement levels for all groups of K–12 students in public schools;
4. The advocacy, politics, and policies affect the average and above average students; and
5. Exploring teacher training, supervision, and program design, comparing results for students in separate versus mainstream (inclusionary) classrooms.

This book is unique, as it examines (in the first chapter) the history of public and special education in the United States as a way to understand just how the situation has developed from past virtual isolation and ignoring of poor, minority, and disabled students. Once we see and analyze the background of the problem, the book examines how court challenges (e.g., *Brown v. Board of Education*) and legislation (PL 94–142, the Education of All Handicapped Children Act) developed and how, meanwhile, parents, advocacy groups, and special educators changed the focus from educating the white, middle-class, English speakers, to those special children who had long been ignored.

We then move to the school level, focusing on school leaders, curriculum, and practices. The final section of the book explores the implications of current and potential future programs and policies and makes suggestions to benefit children at all levels. This book is a valuable tool for educators, parents, and political reformers who are sadly watching American schools deteriorate nationally and internationally. Already, with about 13 percent of children in U.S. schools found to be best served in special education, we are spending over 25 percent of education time on these kids, while ignoring the brightest children who will pass state tests anyway (National Center for Education Statistics, 2014). How long can this go on?

REFERENCES

Friend, M., & Bursuck, W. (1999). *Including students with special needs: A practical guide for classroom teachers*. Needham Heights, MA: Prentice Hall.

National Center for Education Statistics. (2014). Children and Youth with Disabilities.

National Dissemination Center for Children with Disabilities. (2010). Retrieved from http://nichcy.org/schoolage/placement/placement-lre.

Organization for Economic Co-operation and Development (OECD).

Patton, S. (2013). Influx of foreign students drives modest increase in graduate programs. *Chronicle of Higher Education*. September 12. Retrieved from https://chronicle.com/article/Graduate-School-Enrollments/141577/.

Program for International Student Assessment (PISA). 2009.

ONE

History of U.S. Special Education

Bruce S. Cooper and Janet D. Mulvey

Equity has been a driving force for educational movements since Horace Mann proposed education for the masses in 1837, establishing the concept of universal, free public education. Each subsequent era, in its own way, has attempted to guarantee equity to more and different groups in the American population. Constitutional amendments have been used to reinforce equality in education for all.

For example, the court decision *Brown v. Board of Education* (1954), overturned the "separate but equal" clause, citing that segregation based on color was inherently unequal and unconstitutional.

The Civil Rights Law of 1964 bolstered Lyndon B. Johnson's Elementary and Secondary Education Act (ESEA) to provide federal funds, initiating Title I and bilingual programs for children of poverty. And for students with disabilities, the 1974 Education for All Handicapped Children Act (PL 94–142) required all public schools to provide a "free and appropriate education" in the "least restrictive environment" for children with a wide range of disabilities. IDEA (Individuals with Disabilities Education Act) was reauthorized in 2008, mandating services, including extra personnel and resources to assure the best education possible for students with disabilities within public and nonprofit institutions funded by taxes.

Then, this book examines the consequences of full inclusion on the average and above average student in the classroom. At the heart of the discussion is the effectiveness for developing higher-level thinking skills in the unlabeled child. Curricular needs and mandates should be focused on the success of all children, but too often these policies result in teaching to the lower-achieving children to assure their passing state tests. The

1

arguments in this book are not contrary to meeting the needs of students with disabilities but addresses the needs of the "others" in the classroom, ranging from the "regular" education to the talented and highly able kids.

The book then moves to the school level, focusing on the importance of school leadership (e.g., principals and assistant principals) that may be mandated schoollevel programs of inclusionary practices, and their implications. And then, the book looks at classrooms practices, specifically at programs that actually work with children with disabilities within the regular classroom. What are these inclusionary programs and what do they specifically do and address?

We then see how principals, at all levels, manage their schools to ensure success for regular school—and the classrooms' responsiveness to the need for appropriate education for all. Using case studies of particular school leaders, analysis will be done. The central focus rests on the basic principle in the Individuals with Disabilities Education Act (IDEA), our most important federal law for educating students with disabilities.

The law states that special needs children should receive education in the "least restrictive environment" (LRE). This chapter will look at the beliefs that inclusion in a regular classroom is the only appropriate placement for a child with disabilities and will challenge one to think about a "continuum of placements based on the nature and severity of the handicap." This chapter explores how leaders initiate and support curricula to challenge general education students while reinforcing the needs of children with disabilities in public school classrooms.

This study also investigates the move toward inclusion and mainstreaming, for the Education of All Handicapped Children guarantees students with handicapping conditions a free and appropriate education in the least restrictive environment. What does the "least restrictive environment" mean? Pressures mandate continued and increased inclusion of special education children in the general education classroom. This move toward inclusion raises some important questions:

1. What is meant by inclusion?
2. When is inclusion appropriate for students?
3. To what degree are schools sacrificing one student's education for another's?
4. What are the social and academic benefits for students in a common inclusive environment?
5. What are the costs of placing students with disabilities in general education classes both to the children with disabilities and those unclassified?

We then turn our attention to the important issue of teacher training for the twenty-first century, including some proposed core standards for global competency and competitiveness. The qualities set forth by the

American Association of Colleges for Teacher Training use language that clearly states the need for these skills but does not specify what these skills are. Core principles, as outlined, assure teachers' knowledge in promoting inquiry, child development, diversity, critical thinking and performance skills, learning environments, communication skills, assessment, and collaborative environments.

Proficiency and the ability to implement the above principles call for college classrooms that engage the same principles and encourage individual inquiry, engagement, and performance. This book then examines the hopes of standardized curricula and the fallacies it presents for all students' learning styles and cognitive development.

WHERE TO EDUCATE CHILDREN WITH NEEDS

The reauthorization of the No Child Left Behind Act (2008) has reemphasized the policy of integrating students with special needs into the general education classroom. According to the United States Department of Education (2006), approximately 80 percent of students with disabilities receive educational support in the general education classroom.

While teaching to diverse populations of learners may be ideal—being judged as proficient (or not) solely based on standardized tests—it results in lowering standards on general education students to assure passing levels by all in the classroom.

University education programs promote and prescribe pedagogical practices that embrace "differentiated" teaching/learning. This pedagogical approach requires teachers to adjust their lesson plans to meet the individual potentials and learning styles of students in the classroom. The objective for differentiated instruction cannot be argued with. Its positive goal is lofty but too often unrealistic. Preparing lesson strategies, content, and implementation for all learners presupposes that remediation for slower learners, content support for average learners, and enrichment for above average learners can be met in a prescribed period of time.

Students in the average and above average range need maturity to work independently and often have difficulty adjusting to flexible teaching schedules. Thus, while the concept of differentiation seems doable, reality oftentimes presents a different story for the average and above average students in an inclusive classroom. Thus, we explore the assumptions of differentiated teaching, its effectiveness, and the practical implications.

This book then examines some alternatives for ensuring the best possible education for all students. At issue is our failing to meet and enhance the learning opportunities for the "middle child," the average student who needs more attention to develop proficiency and mastery in their learning experiences and potential. Research-based evidence re-mains inconclusive. Thus, it is imperative we listen to the voices of general and special education teachers to clarify our understanding, develop strategies, and improve instruction for all.

FUNDING PROGRAMS FOR ALL CHILDREN

Containing costs and using funds more effectively for all students are the twin problems discussed in this book. We know that the classification and the support of more children with special needs and disabilities have raised the cost of education. With about 13 percent of students now "classified" and needing special attention, the costs for serving these students has reached 24 percent in some districts, while regular education children has actually decline in some urban districts (Hoag, 2012).

As *Huffpost Education* recently reported:

> In Cleveland, the district has lost 41 percent of its students since 1996 while its proportion of students with special needs rose from 13.4 percent to 22.9 percent last year. In Milwaukee, enrollment has dropped by nearly 19 percent over the past decade, but the percentage of students with disabilities has risen from 15.8 percent in 2002 to 19.7 percent in 2012. (Hoag, 2012)

So while costs have risen, the number of regular and gifted children has actually declined. This book analyzes the trends and shows what can be done to serve all students better, more economically, and more effectively in the future.

FINAL THOUGHTS AND SUGGESTIONS

Appropriate mainstream, cooperative team teaching, with both regular and special education working closely together is the best solution to create authentic, project-based learning for all students.

The American Association of Colleges for Teacher Education (AACTE) advisory group and the strategic council of the Partnership for 21st Century Skills have approved the following core principles, representing a shared vision for integrating twenty-first-century skills into educator preparation:

1. P–12 education will prepare all students with twenty-first-century knowledge and skills.
2. P–12 teachers and administrators will possess, teach and assess twenty-first-century knowledge and skills.
3. Educator preparation programs will prepare their graduates to possess, teach and assess twenty-first-century knowledge and skills.

4. New teachers will be prepared to become change agents for embedding twenty-first-century knowledge and skills in all subjects in P–12 curricula in accordance with national and state standards.
5. Higher education leaders will work with leaders in P–12 and local communities to inform the redesign of educator preparation programs to more effectively meet the needs of twenty-first-century learners.
6. Each educator preparation program will develop a twenty-first-century blueprint for transforming itself into a twenty-first-century program.
7. Educator preparation programs will be recognized as sources of leadership in developing twenty-first-century education and learning strategies.
8. Educator preparation programs will be at the forefront of research and evaluation of twenty-first-century education. (AACTE, 2010)

Court Cases

Regarding discrimination against special needs children, IDEA (PL 94–142) establishes children's rights to education, where they were often separated in "special education schools," and later integrated in separate classes but housed in the same, regular schools. The "mainstreaming" approach involved their placement in a regular education classroom for their strong subjects and then returned to special classrooms for support for their needs for these students' disabilities.

Next, in an attempt to teach students together, schools sometimes placed two teachers in the same classroom, one for traditional teaching and the other with more experience working with and supporting the needs of special education students. Meanwhile, the regular education teachers focused on the average and above-average students, in content areas—but working in the same room.

Now, however, the so-called inclusionary model places regular and special education children together, with little or no extra support in same classroom, with the regular education teacher. We discuss how placing students with disabilities into the general education classroom with no support negatively affects the teaching-learning process for all children. Teachers spend more time correcting disruptive behavior or attempting to remediate the learning of children with special needs, thus, paying less attention (having less time available) to children with more potential.

"As the evidence for neurodiversity accumulates, it seems increasingly likely that an overall cure from neurological differences is not possible," reports one author with Asperger's explains. He goes on to question, "Why are we subjecting our students with neurological differences to ineffective learning situations?" (Robison, 2007)

Another observer wrote: "Many successful practices have been re-searched and identified. Special education professionals and parents alike are concerned that regular education teachers have neither the time nor the expertise to meet their [special education children's] needs." (Lyon and Vaughn, 1994).

CONCLUSION

We are seeking to show and understand just how a nation can move from various levels of segregation into full inclusion with the best education for all, regardless of children's race, income, language, and ability. This book is searching for a key idea about our schools: *Equity for all; a challenging, useful education for all; and in one system for all.*

REFERENCES

American Association of Colleges for Teacher Education (AACTE) (2010). 21st Century knowledge and skills in educator preparation. Washington, DC.

Hoag, C. (2012). Students with special needs staying in traditional public schools. In: Huff Post Education, http://www.huffingtonpost.com/2012/08/20/special-needs-kids-stayin_0_n_1803753.html.

Lyon, R., and Vaughn, S. (1994). Inclusion: Can it work for students with learning disabilities? In: *SEDL Concerns about and arguments against inclusion or full inclusion*, Vol 4, No. 3, Inclusion: the pros and cons.

Robison, J. E. (2007). *Look me in the eye*. New York: Random House.

Robison, J. E. (2013). My life with Asperger's. *Psychology Today*. October 7. Retrieved from www.psychologytoday.com.

TWO

What about Me?

Janet D. Mulvey

In the twenty-first century, education is about project-based learning, connections with peers around the world, service learning, independent research, design and creativity, and more than anything else, critical thinking and challenges to old assumptions. —Prakash Nair (2012)

This chapter examines the consequences of full inclusion on the average and above average student in the classroom. At the heart of the discussion is the effectiveness of current policies supporting more inclusion for the labeled child but neglect for developing higher-level thinking skills in the unlabeled child. Meeting curricular needs and mandates should be focused on the success of all children but too often result in teaching to the lower-achieving child to assure passing a test. The argument in this chapter is not contrary to meeting the needs of students with disabilities but addresses the needs of the "other" in the classroom.

Suffice it to say the original intent of the IDEA (Individuals with Disabilities Education Act) was to correct the history of neglect for children with special needs. We do not argue that children who are classified disabled but cognitively bright should be included in the regular classroom but instead take issue that children who are not capable of curricula content and practices distract and interfere with demands of general education.

SPECIAL EDUCATION LEGISLATION IMPACT

President Ford signed legislation more than twenty-five years ago to assure equity for children with special educational needs. The historic legislation ended the exclusion of students with disabilities, giving them a just and equitable opportunity for an education. The early practice of separate classrooms with mainstreaming, when deemed appropriate, has been altered. Currently the trend is to include children (with exception) in the regular classroom with general education populations. The result: curricula in too many classrooms has been simplified, leaving the average child unchallenged to reach his or her potential. Critics of current inclusion policy have been admonished and accused of being uncaring and secular. Finn, Rotherham, and Hokanson (2001) state, "well-intentioned people who have attempted to highlight deficiencies, inequities, and problems with special education have been criticized as interlopers with bad motives or political agendas and told to leave such matters to the stakeholder community" (p. v).

We feel it is time to examine all aspects of both special and regular education to benefit all our students in the public school systems. How do we assure the best education possible for all 55,235,000 students in our K–12 public schools? (National Center for Educational Statistics, 2011).

INTERNATIONAL STANDING

International educational ranking in the United States continues to suffer from less-than-stellar performance. The Program for International Student Assessment (PISA) is an international assessment that measures fifteen-year-old students' reading, mathematics, and science literacy. The test also uses measures of competencies across curricula areas and compares readiness of students internationally as they near the end of compulsory education. The last test administered was in 2012.

Many of our public school students fall short in all areas on the PISA. American students, for example, place fourteenth in literacy and twenty-fourth in math internationally (OECD, 2013). We continue to lag behind countries with "third world" designations. Policy makers, government officials, and educators should be embarrassed by our poor performance but seem unable to overcome the political pressures placed on them by advocacy groups and voting lobbies. Teaching to higher standards includes authentic application with critical thinking and problem solving and challenging students to reach their highest potential. Simplifying curriculum, teaching to tests, and lowering expectations for students is a formula for failure.

According to Jeanne St. Germaine's *Horizontal Congruence of Assessments/Audits and Deliverables* (2011):

> The rational and logical approach of best practices in global education needs to replace emotional arrogance that prevails in American education. The reality is not that students need to get used to heterogeneous groups. The reality is that U.S. education consistently ranks lowest in

comparison with other countries. If the United States does not reprioritize its approach to education (e.g., inclusion), our population will not be prepared to compete in the global economy presented by formerly third world countries. (p. 6)

How do we remove the political influences for special education from the docket and do what is best for our students? How can we create effective performance-enhanced schooling?

THE EFFECTIVE SCHOOL AND STUDENT

Effective school research aligns success with several environmental characteristics: "high expectations for all students, challenging curricula across the board, enriched teaching and learning with 'minds-on' engagement, professional development, and involvement of parents and community" (Langer, 2004). Quality instruction based on cognitive demand, engagement, and continual assessment requires a teacher's ability to challenge her class and teach to a level greater than standardized test formats. Bergeson (2007) states,

> While the deep alignment between what is taught and tested with the state standards is critical, effective instruction is key to reaching state standards . . . impact of deeply aligning the content, context and cognitive demand of curriculum, instruction and assessment cannot be overstated. (p. 9)

Placing special education students into the regular classroom can compromise the rights of the average and above average students. Premised on the type of disability, students who may be hyperactive, neurologically or perceptually impaired, or disruptive can upset the performance potential of the regular education student. Leadley (2004) writes, "When neurologically or perceptually impaired students are thrown into the mix, they often occupy a disproportionate amount of the classroom teachers' time. . . . Thus the education of the regular population is unfairly hampered when the special needs students monopolize a teacher's time" (np).

Cognitively lower students need more teacher-directed attention. Their focus and engagement must be addressed often, taking time from a curriculum flow and interrupting thought processes of the "others" in the classroom. If we imagine a social studies class on the Bill of Rights and set up a hypothetical scenario creating a violation of those rights, do we stop the flow of reaction and spontaneity for a literal translation and explanation? Do we scale down the activity and lose the engagement of the more cognitively able students?

St. Germaine (2011) explains:

Students with these limited capacities require consistent stimulation and motivation, demanding more of the teacher's time and effort. These particular students need smaller teaching steps and more remediation—an entirely different method of teaching. In comparison, higher functioning students can become bored and also begin to exhibit behavioral issues. (p. 4)

Finland, the number one country on international assessments, has compulsory schooling for all its children. Preschool is mandated for all. Students identified as needing intensive support are provided it as early as possible. They are provided all services necessary to help them complete as much of a comprehensive education as possible. They are not required to take every general subject and are given special training after primary and middle school.

A statistical comparison of students with disabilities from *Ed Data Express* shows similar percentages, with 11.4 percent for Finland (2011) and 12.8 percent for the United States (2009) (Snyder & Dillow, 2011). In Finland, 99.2 percent of students attend public school, and 89 percent do in the United States. While students with disabilities can be in the regular education program, in Finland they are provided every service to receive and not distract the learning of general educational pupils. As Janet Mulvey (2011) comments,

The learning climate in Finland schools supports the whole child, physically, psychologically, and socially. The objective is to increase motivation, curiosity to learn and become self-directed through challenging and problem solving curricula . . . [and] adhere to the mission by allowing students to pursue alternative ways to fulfill desired goals. (pp. 42–43)

Students in Finland and other European countries do not neglect their students with special needs but assure educational success according to need and ability. The result, a consistent first place in international educational ranking and a dropout rate of less than 1 percent. Students, when asked, say they love school and that learning is enjoyable and teachers don't waste so much time on testing but on teaching.

DROPPING OUT: SCHOOL AND SOCIETY

The dropout rate from our nation's high schools has risen two years in a row (Bridgeland, Dilulio, & Morison, 2006). Wealth of district resources and supports has an influence on the number. Wealthier districts provide extra resources for all students, with extra support and tutoring for those with special needs. Poorer districts have few resources, resulting in less support for students with or without special needs. The poorer the district, the greater the disconnect from school, thus, the larger the dropout rate. Overall, approximately 7,200 students leave high school on a daily basis, or 1.3 million per year (Bridgeland, Dilulio, & Morison, 2006). Lack of effective instruction, student engagement, cognitive stimulation, and professional development create few reasons to remain in school for many of our students.

Table 2.1 shows the consistency of dropouts in ethnic groups, where fewer resources, support, and services exist. It is also well documented that public schools in high-poverty but minority-rich districts identify learning disabilities for fewer students than wealthy districts but place more special education students into inclusive settings. The conundrum is twofold: (1) Less wealth in low socioeconomic areas results in fewer special education service availability, providing less remediation. (2) Fewer teachers and paraprofessionals result in more students with disabilities in the general education setting.

Matthew Ladner and Christopher Hammons (2001) sum it up:

> The data indicate that the percentage of minority students in a district is the driving force in determining special education rates. . . . Districts with high percentages of minority students—regardless of whether they are urban or rural, rich or poor—actually tend to place fewer students in special education programs. (p. 98)

Karen, a high school social studies teacher in an urban school, has left her position from the stress of feeling unable to meet the needs of her students. Alone in a large, crowded, inner-city classroom, 40 percent of her students have IEP (Individualized Education Plans). Her principal, concerned with the rating of the school and its possible closure, emphasized passing the regents for all students, negating anything but test preparation for a good part of the year. The 60 percent general education students became, according to Karen, less engaged, more truant, and less tolerant with their special needs peers (teaching.monster.com).

Laura, an elementary first-grade teacher, complains how difficult—if not impossible—it is to ready her young students for literacy and math skills when she spends so much time controlling six students with aggressive behaviors. Five boys and one girl have significant behavioral issues that interfere with normal classroom routine. Her remaining students are distracted and often frightened by the uncontrolled outbursts. Classified and with individual education plans, these six students are entitled by law to have services to control their behaviors while teaching basic readiness skills. Laura is concerned. Her remaining twenty students are already experiencing the negative effects of unfair inclusion, affecting improvement for both special needs and general education students. How will they be ready to reach mandated standards and assessments?

Effective school systems require combinations of resources, trained professional teachers and administrators, well-developed facilities, and motivated students. An analysis from the international committee finds that only Luxembourg spends more money per pupil than the United

Table 2.1.   Status Dropout Rates of Sixteen- through Twenty-Four-Year-Olds in the Civilian, Noninstitutionalized Population, by Race/Ethnicity. Selected Years, 1990–2010. *Source: U.S. Department of Education, National Center for Education Statistics. (2012).* **The Condition of Education, 2012 (NCES 2012–045), Table A-3.**

Year	Total		Race/Ethnicity				
		White	Black	Hispanic		Asian/ Pacific Islander	American Indian/ Alaskan Native
1990	12.1	9.0	13.2	32.4		4.91	16.41
1995	12.0	8.6	12.1	30.0		3.9	13.41
1998	11.8	7.7	13.8	29.5		4.1	11.8
1999	11.2	7.3	12.6	28.6		4.3	
2000	10.9	6.9	13.1	27.8		3.8	14.0
2001	10.7	7.3	10.9	27.0		3.6	13.1
2002	10.5	6.5	11.3	25.7		3.9	16.8
2003	9.9	6.3	10.9	23.5		3.9	15.0
2004	10.3	6.8	11.8	23.8		3.6	17.0
2005	9.4	6.0	10.4	22.4		2.9	14.0
2006	9.3	5.8	10.7	22.1		3.6	14.7
2007	8.7	5.3	8.4	21.4		6.1	19.3
2008	8.0	4.8	9.9	18.3		4.4	14.6
2009	8.1	5.2	9.3	17.6		3.4	13.2
2010	7.4	5.1	8.0	15.1		4.2	12.4

States. Yet after primary school, inefficiencies in secondary schools result in ranking our country behind countries who spend far less (OECD, 2010).

We argue that socioeconomic inequities in education are but one reason for our overall failure on the PISA, and inclusion resulting in teaching to lower standards with less motivation for the average and above student are equally at fault. Analysis of achievement across the socio economic strata shows how quality in resources, facility, teacher training, and expertise differ. Also true is the fact that children who live in poorer communities have more students with disabilities in their general education classrooms.

In New York City alone, the schools that rank the highest have the fewest special education students in their classrooms. Teachers in these schools have the opportunity to teach higher-level skills, move at a faster pace, and allow more authentic projects for student engagement and learned problem-solving strategies. A report by Fertig (2012) refers to an analysis done by WNYC, which "found that high schools with the best report card grades often take smaller percentages of the special education students who are the toughest to educate . . . less than 2 percent of their overall population."

With a large percentage of students in urban settings with fewer resources, changes in policy are imperative. Preparing students for future participation in a democratic, social, and economically prosperous society means giving them the best and highest standard of education possible. Burdening the less wealthy student with the more difficult classrooms, lower standards, and fewer possibilities for success undermines the purpose of public education.

COLLEGE READINESS IN THE UNITED STATES

Too many of our high school graduates are unprepared for the rigors of college curricula. Our international standing remains below par for competiveness in the global marketplace. A 2012 report from ACT, Inc., reveals the results of high school graduates who have selected college as the next step in their education. The following graph is an indicator of our strengths and weaknesses on the ACT.

While 67 percent of those who took the test met the benchmarks for English, a downward trend is apparent in reading, math, and science. For complete readiness in all four subjects, 25 percent of test takers met the benchmarks for success.

College readiness requires students to be proficient in high school classes in order to acquire necessary knowledge and skills for success in higher-level education. Students must have literacy skills to meet all con-

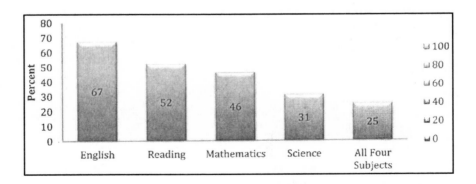

Figure 2.1.   Percent of ACT-Tested High School Graduates Meeting College Readiness Benchmarks by Subject, 2012. Source: Graph from ACT, Inc., College Readiness Benchmarks by Subject.

tent areas, and have the cognitive abilities to think critically and problem solve. The public school should be the venue to prepare students for college or career-centered, post-secondary learning. Reports by Jay Greene and Greg Forster (2003) indicate what "education policy makers are increasingly concerned with is that too many graduates aren't college ready. There is a gap between what high schools require for graduation and . . . what four year colleges require" (p. 3).

An alarming report by Hildebrand (2013), indicates, "State school officials confirmed . . . that percentages of students passing new, more rigorous English and math tests could drop by nearly half . . . cutting success rates as low as 35 percent statewide" (np). Percentage of students passing new state tests could drop.

If dropout rates lower high school graduation by 30 percent and 32 percent of those who do graduate are not college ready, how do we remediate our policies to improve our chances for a progressive and educated twenty-first-century citizenry?

Sir Ken Robinson (2012) author and lecturer, refers to our education system as antiquated and uninspiring. He states, "We're all born with deep natural capacities for creativity and mass education tends to suppress them" (np).

Students placed in classrooms where creativity is stifled, where applications are nonexistent, and where experience is limited to making sure all pass a test is testament to our shortcomings in preparing students for college and postsecondary education. How can we compete globally if we are ill prepared for the demands of the future?

It is prudent to break prevailing mental models that exist only in the United States and explore/utilize best practices identified on a global scale. Every student does have the right to a free public education; this is not congruent with mandating inclusive classrooms. As Leadley (2004) so aptly summarizes,

> A special education student should certainly be granted access to the regular education classroom if he or she is capable of performing without any undue modifications. . . . The educational opportunities of the regular education student should not be stifled in any in an inane attempt to stroke the ego of the minority interests. (np)

SPECIAL EDUCATION POLICIES TIME LINE

Throughout the twentieth century the field of special education repeatedly adopted instructional strategies of questionable efficacy interventions that have little to no empirical basis. Additionally, special educators have adopted, with bandwagon fervor, many practices that have been proven ineffective and have thereby repeated the mistakes of history. If special education is to progress, professionals will need to address and remedy the instructional practices used with students with disabilities. Students without the cognitive ability to achieve mastery in the regular classroom should not retard the learning of those who do. Laws requiring a least restrictive environment (LRE) means requiring the environment best suited for the learning needs of the student. It does not mean a setting with the fewest restrictions or assistance.

Public schools have been experiencing an ever-increasing influx of students classified with learning disabilities into their classrooms. According to the Rehabilitation Research and Training Center on Disability Statistics and Demographics at Hunter College (2009), estimates range from 10.8 percent for ages three to five to 43.3 percent for ages twelve to seventeen years of age. The data represents all disabilities: academic, mental, physical, emotional, and behavioral.

Students with the most severe disabilities are more often educated in separate facilities or rooms within the public school. The estimate for children with disabilities in inclusive classrooms within the public school setting in grades K–I2 is 12.8 percent. And the No Child Left Behind (NCLB) Act, established in 2001, mandates that 95 percent of students with disabilities in the general education settings take standardized tests. The scores are reported and analyzed to determine the rating and ranking of the school, placing emphasis on passing the test.

Revision of IDEA to IDEIA (Individuals with Disabilities Education Improvement Act) has resulted, according to Baker and Zigmond (1995) in "the abandonment of pull-out programs and return of students to the general education setting while delivering whatever instruction is needed within the confines of the general education classroom" (p. 172). Federal laws have been driving state education rules and exert more oversight into every aspect of states' public school systems. The federal NCLB Act mandates that schools demonstrate proficiency in literacy and math or face being labeled "failing" and possibly being closed. The NCLB mandate also requires students with disabilities to be included in standardized assessments. And according to Robinson (2012), "students classified as special education are deemed a mandatory 'sub group,' a schools success or failure depends upon the standardized assessment scores of the special education population" (np).

Parents of children with disabilities do not have to supply burden of proof that their child can function in a regular education classroom. In a 1993 case, *Oberti v. Board of Education of the Borough of Clementon School District*, a U.S. circuit court ruled that Raphael Oberti, a student with Down syndrome had the legal right to attend his neighborhood school. It determined that resources he needed to be successful must be implemented in the general education classroom. The judge in the case maintained failure on part of the school district to provide appropriate training for teachers and staff within the school. Compliance with inclusion requirements was placed squarely on the school district and the state.

The parents had no responsibility in proving whether their son could succeed in the setting. Complicit in the ruling, however, was the institution of aids and services in the general education classroom. "The school had to show why this student could not be educated in general education with aids and services, and his family did not have to prove why he could. The federal judge who decided the case stated, 'Inclusion is a right, not a special privilege for a select few'" (Kluth, Villa, & Thousand, 2001/2002, np).

This ruling did not suppose that the student could succeed without the proper supports. Instead the ruling clearly indicated the need for appropriate supports, allowing the student to participate but not distract from the learning of the others in the classroom.

Under IDEA (Individuals with Disabilities Education Act), children identified with disabilities must be given a free and appropriate public education. They are to be mainstreamed or included into the general education classroom whenever possible. The question for us to consider is should we also identify the needs of the average or above average student whose potential is not being fulfilled because of focus on meeting mandates for students with disabilities? The average and above average student has been ignored for too long. We are evidencing the results with lower achievement rates across the board. How do we provide an education to meet their potential?

IMPLEMENTATION AND CONSEQUENCES

What are the exact mandates and how are they interpreted among schools and districts? The intent of equality in education is built on the essence of what constitutes equality and freedom. Macmurray (1950) presupposes:

> If we do not treat one another as equals, we exclude freedom from the relationship. Freedom too conditions equality. For if there is restraint between us, there is fear; and to counter the fear we must seek control over its object, and attempt to subordinate the other person to our own power. Any attempt to achieve freedom without equality, or to achieve equality without freedom, must, therefore be self-defeating. (p. 74)

Macmurray's approach has been used to argue the rights of students with disabilities in the public school and classroom. There is no argument that all Americans should be given their constitutional rights of freedom and equal opportunity. Thus opportunity applies to all students in every classroom, students with and without disabilities. One parent wrote, "I feel strongly that my children in regular classrooms have a civil right to learn without having their paths to progress disrupted and diverted by the demands of a disabled child" (Kastens, 1995, p. A15).

Parents and school districts are not well educated on the law and its interpretation when it comes to inclusive classroom settings. Receiving a free and appropriate education should not result in ignoring or neglecting the general education students in the classroom. The law is clear:

> To the maximum extent appropriate, children with disabilities . . . are educated with children who are not disabled, and special classes, separate schooling, or other removal of children with disabilities from the regular education environment occurs only when the nature or severity of the disability . . . is such that education in regular classes with the use of supplementary aids and services cannot be achieved satisfactorily. (20 U.S.C., 1412[5][A])

Courts have held that educating a disabled child in general education (LRE), while preferable, is secondary to ensuring the child receives a free and appropriate public education (FAPE). Also stressed with inclusion is the "use of supplementary aids and services," freeing the general education teacher to hold the curriculum to standards achievable by average and above average students.

Many books advocate for full inclusion, and parents continue to support access to general education classrooms, and understandably so. In her article "Facts and Falacies: Differentiation and the General Education Curriculum for Students with Special Education Needs," Margaret King-Sears (2008) resoundingly supports practices where students can prosper. KingSears, a strong supporter for inclusive settings, also concedes:

> General educators feeling pressure to cover so much content with so many students' learning levels and at a swift pace are understandably overwhelmed. On top of that, they and their administrators are anxious about the high-stakes consequences when their students do not show adequate yearly progress on large-scale assessments. It is not sufficient, although it is important, that techniques amplify the growth of students with disabilities and students who are at risk for school failure. It is equally important that the techniques accelerate learning for average students and students who are higher achievers. (p. 57)

BOREDOM AND APATHY

Students in high school often lament how boring classes are when content is simplified to assure students with less potential are able to understand and pass tests. Instead of being engaged in authentic and discovery curriculum, a week is spent on a single concept (already learned by the general education student) that may be on a test all students in the inclusive setting have to pass. This lack of attention to the needs of the "other" in the classroom results in the poor statistics of readiness for postsecondary education for those students with potential.

Teachers are too often compelled to slow the pace of instruction, simplify basic concepts, ignore higher-level thinking skills, and challenge discovery instincts and curiosity.

Kayla Webley (2012) comments, "There's a reason why colleges have to remediate so many students. According to a report on college and career readiness from the ACT, . . .the latest results of the organization's standardized college entrance test, only 1 in 4 students qualify in all four subject areas: English, reading, math and science" (np).

Education has, in too many instances, become a boring nonstimulating legal obligation until the age of sixteen. *Education Week* (Sparks, 2012) cites statistics indicating that 65 percent of students are bored in school, at least some of the time. If, as Armstrong (2012) believes, "school is for awakening the mind, not putting it to sleep," (np) we need to revolt and change direction from test-driven, standards-based instruction to a more Socratic method of dialectal discovery.

Have we discriminated against our brighter students and violated the law by not giving them a "free and appropriate education"? What is appropriate, and for whom? Why is there no hue and cry over the lack of "appropriate" education for the average student in a classroom where 40 percent of students may have special education needs, especially in poorer and underfunded districts? Robert Worth (1999) cites the inequity of funding for the general education student as well as the cost-cutting alternatives that too often fall on the backs of the average plus student: "Unlike general education, special education is a federal mandate: School districts can be sued (and routinely are) for not providing every service parents think is appropriate for their kids" (np).

School districts must comply with federal mandates, although there is little empirical evidence supporting many of the intervention practices, including inclusion, as effective for students with disabilities. According to Kauffman (1999) too many special educators have adopted a bandwagon mentality, adopting practices that are ineffective. Inclusion is a practice that continues to be questioned for its effectiveness for students with disabilities as well as a detriment for the regular education student.

FINANCIAL COSTS

Costs to districts for special education services can be onerous. Students within severe ranges of needs and low cognitive and trainable abilities who are placed in special settings can cost sixty thousand dollars or more annually. Public schools spend at least double or triple the amount as compared to the general education student. Students who cannot be placed within the district public school must be transported to special facilities with extra supports such as PT (physical therapy), OT (occupational therapy), and so on. According to the National Education Association (2004):

> Public schools across the country today serve more than six million children with a wide array of disabling conditions. Ever since the enactment of the Individuals with Disabilities Education Act, the federal law has included a commitment to pay 40 percent of the average per student cost for every special education student. However, 2004 statistics showed that the federal government paid only 20 percent of their commitment. The burden is on communities and states to pay the rest. (np)

Bauer (1994) recognized the financial implications of the inclusive classroom as it became more practiced and implemented in the public school setting. Advocates for inclusion never addressed the costs. As Bauer explains:

> There is little evidence that those who advocate inclusion recognize the need to reduce class size considerably . . . [or] the need for larger and larger numbers of teachers; and the consequent expense such numbers would entail. This is precisely what those who advocate inclusion would like to avoid. (p. 23)

With rising costs of education, placing more special education students within district public schools is a financial necessity. However, it is not always educationally sound for regular education students. Poor children, with special needs or not, are placed into classrooms without the necessary financial supports due to budget constraints. Each is a victim, and neither has the chance to reach potential. Special education is a government mandate and cannot be ignored by school districts, wealthy or poor. The difference is in the ability to raise money to obey the legal mandate and to educate the more cognitively able.

Worth (1999) states succinctly, "In order to pay for special ed's enormous, ineffectual, and skyrocketing enrollments, school districts are being forced to cheat their conventional students" (np).

WORKING FOR THE UNLABELED

Teachers recognize the need for differentiation in heterogeneously grouped classrooms. None expect all students to learn the same way and develop lessons based on learning theories and strategies. Without assistance in a classroom to meet the special needs of students with moderate or more severe disabilities, even the best teachers cannot comply with all that is required. As G. M. Chesley and P. D. Calaluce (1997) express:

> "I have twenty-five children in my second-grade class, and you can't expect me to take on more students with special needs" has become the oft-heard plea school after school. This carries some grain of truth to

even the most hard-core supporters of inclusion and illustrates a legiti-
mate road-block to a full inclusionary model. (p. 489)

Inclusion advocates use the law and studies for inclusion maintaining all
students learn best in classrooms with differentiated instruction and
common goals. Evidence from other research maintains they are compelled by evidence of research, but studies actually show that low-achiev-
ing students in mixed-ability classrooms become self-conscious when
working alongside classmates with higher ability. Rather than becoming
encouraged by learning, students with lower ability become withdrawn
and rely on the more proficient students to be participatory and provide
the answers. Tom Loveless (1999) states, "The mixed-ability classrooms
that result from de-tracking may force low achievers into daily compari-
sons with their more able peers, conditions hostile to the development of
self-confidence" (p. 16).

The National Research Council issued a report on the lack of student
motivation in 2003. Students unmotivated and consistently disengaged
are candidates for either failure and/or dropping out. Raising standards
and prepping for assessments have done little to change the outcome and
have, in fact, contributed to negative results in achievement and performance. Teachers who are mandated by school administrators to prepare
for city, state, and federal tests, have little time to execute motivating
lessons. Exacerbating the situation is the NCLB Act, mandating 95 percent of students with special needs in inclusive settings must take the
same assessments.

Teachers are chronically using test-driven materials from publishing
houses that guarantee passing standards to assure all students in the
inclusive classroom achieve minimum requirements. The scores are published, providing false information on the knowledge and mastery in all
subject areas. Compounding the lack of preparation for realistic knowledge skills, students who are cognitively ready for challenging and inter-
esting material are subjected to the worst kind of boredom.

Creci asserts, "Students who are bored or inattentive or who put little
effort to schoolwork are chronically disengaged . . . [and] are unlikely to
benefit from better standards, curriculum and instruction" (National Research Council, 2003). On the other hand, motivation to learn, engagement in lessons, and challenged thinking achieve concept development,
problem solving, and application to new and unfamiliar situations, a
system necessary for the fast pace of information in the twenty-first century.

Researched-based steps to engage and encourage student learning
are:

1. Feeling of competence to engage and complete an assignment
2. Application of information currently and for the future
3. Interest and value to them

4. Successful completion brings validation and reward socially and collegially

While each of these steps can relate to all students, regardless of learning abilities, the inclusive classroom remains focused on the lower achieving student's acquisition, leaving the average to above student unfulfilled.

Teachers expressing their concern wonder how they can meet the needs mandated by IEPs and engage and challenge their "other" students. Battling every day to satisfy and support students with learning needs and instill enthusiasm for conventional students while adhering to test expectations has caused many to leave the profession. Frustration, weariness, and despair have entered the classroom where there should instead be excitement and joy.

The push to include all but the most disabled into the general education setting meets resistance from educators who understand the need to engage the average and above student to learn and complete their education with focus and goals for the future. Gallagher (1994) writes, "There is something amiss in full inclusion plan—that fairness does not consist of educating all children in the same place at the same time" (p. 525).

Schooling has been a mandate since Horace Mann introduced compulsory education in 1836. Unfortunately for those with special needs, neglect, institutionalization, or private schooling was their only means of care, training, and education. The question we raise in this chapter is have we gone so far in recognizing the needs of the student with disabilities and ignoring the imperatives of a challenging education for the average and above student in a traditional setting?

Why should students whose ability is at least average or above be relegated to low-performing classrooms? We are squandering human resources to the detriment of public institutions and society. High achieving students are a necessity to our schools. They are role models for education. They raise scores and have positive impacts on motivation and excitement for learning. And they change the focus from just passing tests to promoting environments for educational exploration, discovery, thinking, and learning.

CONCLUSION

Compulsory education for all is the law of the land until the age of sixteen. Special education is a federal mandate for all types of disabilities. Thus, students with special needs are assured placements in the least restrictive environment. The term itself is confusing and promotes a general misunderstanding of what it means. The intent of the term is to make sure that students with disabilities are placed in an environment where they have the opportunity to reach their potential. It is not intended to place them in an environment with the least supports and services just because it is a general education setting. This practice is unfair to the special student, the traditional student, the teacher, and the school.

School districts are routinely sued (successfully) for placements not fulfilling the parents' and advocates' wishes, who too often misunderstand what is best for the student. The cost to the district in legal fees is massive and results in complying with wishes and inappropriate placements.

Goals established by the Council for Exceptional Children and the National Association of State School Boards of Education contain language that should be a focus for the general education student as well but seems to exclude that intent. For example: "The focus of inclusion should be on the student. Inclusive schools should provide curriculum programs that meet the needs of all students" (Council for Exceptional Children, 1994). Doesn't the traditional student deserve the same consideration?

The costs for special education programs are so massive that school districts have had to tighten their belts for regular education to meet the mandates of IDEA. The federal government promised reimbursement of up to 40 percent for special services and program supports but in reality have only contributed 10 percent. This burden is affecting the quality of classroom instruction for the majority of attending students.

In a southern California district, the cost for special education has grown from three million dollars to eleven million in a little over three years. Worth (1999) recites that "school districts face a painful choice: raise local property taxes or cut back on students. . . . 'We are cannibalizing our regular education budget,' says Joe Quick, an administrator in the Wisconsin public school system. 'For the first time since 1975, teachers are saying "why are those kids here?" . . . It's really starting to drive a wedge between regular ed and special ed'" (p.2).

Now more than ever, our country needs well-educated youth instilled with a love of learning, curiosity, and the confidence to explore and envision future growth possibilities. The mass population must be able to sustain the economic viability of the country, plan for future expansion, and compete globally in all areas of enterprise.

The focus in city, suburban, and rural classroom environments should be to prepare future citizens who are diverse in talents but well educated. We agree there are classified students who can achieve standards mandated by local and state education departments. These students should be part of, and participate in, the regular education program. Leadley (2004) reiterates, "In order to ensure that all students are provided with the best education possible, self-esteem must take a back seat to academics" (np).

The civil rights of those with disabilities and special needs must never be violated, but neither should the civil rights of the traditional student be compromised. Our students are our hope and our future. All should be given equal resources and opportunity to succeed in our public school system. Dropout rates must be mitigated through engagement, interest, and application of what is learned in the classroom to the outside community. And preparation for college or postsecondary education should be looked forward to for self- and societal sustenance.

REFERENCES

ACT, Inc. (2012). College Readiness Benchmarks by Subject.

Armstrong, T. (2012), Bored with school? Sorry kid, deal with it. *American Institute for Learning's Development*. Retrieved from http://institute4learning.com/blog/2012/10/10/bored-with-school-sorry-kid-deal-with-it/.

Baker and Zigmond. (1995). The meaning and practice of inclusion for students with learning disabilities. *Journal of Special Education* 29, 163–190.

Bauer, N. J. (1994). The politics of inclusion: A dissenting paper. Paper presented at the Annual Conference of the New York State Association of Teacher Educators, April 21. Syracuse, NY.

Bergeson, T. (2007). *Nine characteristics of high-performing schools: A research-based resource for schools and districts to assist with improving student learning*. Olympia, WA: Office of Superintendent of Public Instruction.

Bridgeland, J. M., Dilulio, J., & Morison, K. B. (2006). The silent epidemic: Perspectives of high school dropouts. Bill & Melinda Gates Foundation.

Chesley, G. M., & Calaluce, Jr., P. D. (1997). The deception of inclusion. *Mental Retardation, 35*(6), 488–490.

Council for Exceptional Children. (1994). In: Vaughn, S., Schumm, S., & Forgan, J. W. ASCD: *Instructing students with high-incidence disabilities in the general education classroom*.

Digest of Education Statistics. (2010). U.S. Department of Education NCES 2011-015. http://nces.ed.gov/pubsearch/pubsinfo.asp?pubid=2011015.

Fertig, B. (2012). "Do high need students affect a school grade?" WNYC public radio. February 13, 2012.

Finn, C. E., Rotherham, A. J., & Hokanson, C. R. (eds.). (2001). *Rethinking special education for a new century*. Thomas B. Fordham Foundation and the Progressive Policy Institute. Retrieved from http://www.dlc.org/documents/SpecialEd_complete_volume.pdf.

Gallagher, J. J. (1994). The pull of societal focus on special education. *Journal of Special Education, 27*(Winter), 521–530.

Greene, J. P., & Forster, G. F. (2003). *Public high school graduation and college readiness rates in the United States*. Manhattan Institute for Policy Research Working Education Paper No. 3, September.

Hildebrand, J. (2013, April 19). Percentage of students passing new state tests could drop. *Newsday*. Retrieved from http://www.newsday.com/long-island/education/officials-percentage-of-students-passing-new-state-tests-could-drop-1.5041927.

Kastens, T. Y. (1995, January 4). My children have a civil right to learn. *Washington Post*, p. Al5.

Kauffman, J. (1999). Today's special education and its messages for tomorrow. *Journal of Special Education* 32, 244–254.

King-Sears, M. E. (2008). Facts and fallacies: Differentiation and the general education curriculum for students with special education needs. *Support for Learning, 23*(2), 55–62.

Kluth, P., Villa, R. A., & Thousand, J. S. (2001/2002). Our school doesn't offer inclusion and other legal blunders. *Educational Leadership, 59*(4), 24–27. Retrieved from http://www.ascd.org/publications/educational-leadership/dec01/vol59/num04/%C2%A3Our-School-Doesn't-Offer-Inclusion%C2%A3-and-Other-Legal-Blunders.aspx.

Ladner, M., & Hammons, C. (2001). Special but unequal: Race and special education. In C. E. Finn, A. J. Rotherham, & C. R. Hokason (eds.), *Rethinking special education for a new century* (pp. 85–110). Thomas B. Fordham Foundation and Progressive Policy Institute. Retrieved from http://www.dlc.org/documents/SpecialEd_complete_volume.pdf.

Langer, J. A. (2004). *Getting to excellent: How to create better schools.* New York: Teachers College Press.

Leadley, S. (2004, December 8). Placing special ed students in the regular classroom can be detrimental to all. *Intellectual Conservative.* Retrieved from http://www.freerepublic.com/focus/fr/1298994/posts.

Loveless, T. (1999). Will tracking reform promote social equity? *Educational Leadership, 56*(7), 28-32.

Macmurray, J. (1950). *Conditions of freedom.* London: Faber.

Mulvey, J. (2011). Applying Finland's paradigm to NYC kids. *School Administrator, 68*(1), 42–43.

Nair, P. (2012).*New learning environments for 21st century learners.* In: Li, P. P. et al. (2005), "Creating 21st Century Learning Environments," PEB Exchange, Programme on Educational Building, 2005/10 OECD Publishing. http://dx.doi.org/10.1787/558676471016.

National Education Association. (2004). Background of Special education and the Individuals with Disabilities Act: The 2004 IDEA Re-authorization Bill. http://www.nea.org/home/19029.htm.

National Research Council. (2003). *Engaging Schools: Fostering High School Students' Motivation to Learn.* Washington, DC: The National Academies Press.

Oberti v. Board of Education of the Borough of Clementon School District. (1993). 995 F.2d 1204 (3rd Cir.).

OECD. (2010). *OECD factbook 2010: Economic, environmental and social statistics.* OECD Publishing.

OECD. (2013). *OECD factbook 2013: Economic, environmental and social statistics.* OECD Publishing.

Rehabilitation Research and Training Center on Disability Statistics and Demographics at Hunter College. (2009). ResearchonDisability.org. http://www.researchondisability.org.

Robinson, K. (2012, December 7). Do schools kill creativity? *Huffington Post,* Retrieved from http://www.huffingtonpost.com/sir-kenrobinson/do-schools-kill-creativity_b_2252942.html.

Snyder, T. D., & Dillow, S. A. (2011). *Digest of Education Statistics (2010).* Washington, DC: U.S. Dept of Education.

Sparks, S. D. (2012). Studies link students' boredom to stress. *Education Week.* http://www.edweek.org/ew/articles/2012/10/10/boredom.

St. Germaine, J. (2011). *Horizontal congruence of assessments/audits and deliverables.* In: The inclusive classroom model is not efficient or effectice. Pawley Lean Institute. Oakland University, Rochester, MI.

Teaching.monster.com. Achieving Equity in Special Education: History, Status, and Current Challenges. http://teaching.monster.com/benefits/articles/3615-achieving-equity-in-special-education-history-status-and-current-challenges.

Webley, K. (2012, August 24), ACT scores show high school students are not ready for college. *Time News Feed.* Retrieved from http://newsfeed.time.com/2012/08/24/act-scores-show-high-school-students-are-not-ready-for-college/.

Worth, R. (1999). The scandal of special-ed: It wastes money and hurts the poor. *Washington Monthly, 31*(6). Retrieved from http://www.washingtonmonthly.com/features/1999/9906.worth.scandal.html.

THREE

The Principal's Role in Supporting All Students

Karen Gagliardi

Having a disability in no way diminishes the right of individuals to participate or contribute to society. Improving educational results for children with disabilities is an essential element of our national policy of ensuring equality of opportunity, full participation, independent living, and economic self-sufficiency for individuals with disabilities.
—Individuals with Disabilities Education Improvement Act of 2004, as amended

RESPONSIBILITY FOR ALL

The most recent education model to emerge is that of inclusive education. Although the term *inclusion* does not appear in federal laws governing special education, provisions in these laws as other education and civil rights legislation provide a strong foundation for inclusive practices (McLaughlin, 2012). This foundation is unlikely to be abandoned as new laws are enacted. For example, the Individuals with Disabilities Education Act (IDEA) requires that students be educated in the least restrictive environment and the Elementary and Secondary Education Act, (ESEA) mandates access to the curriculum for all students.

Together, these provisions have led state and local policy makers to stress inclusive practices. Similar comments could be made related to provisions such as the requirement for all students to participate in assessments and to make adequate yearly progress (AYP) and those related to teachers being highly qualified in core content areas. This trend is not likely to vanish.

This chapter focuses on the role, responsibility, and challenge of the principal in meeting mandates, providing an equitable education to all, and meeting the needs of students. Educational reformers maintain their commitment to holding all students, including those with disability, to high standards so that they leave school well prepared for college or a vocation (U.S. Department of Education, 2009). Not all the legislative influences are positive, however. For example, the requirements of ESEA have resulted in tremendous pressure for all students to reach achievement goals. In some schools, teachers fear that having students with disabilities in their classes may lower their average class scores. Others note that proposals to link teacher pay to the performance of their students may result in teachers resisting instructing students with disabilities out of concern they may miss out on bonuses and other financial incentives (Gratz, 2009).

Since the term *inclusion* appears to have multiple meanings, it is important to distinguish between inclusion and full inclusion. Proponents of full inclusion believe that there should not be any special education services and that all students with disabilities should be taught in general education classrooms (Fuchs & Fuchs, 1994). Rogers (1994) defines full inclusion as a term "primarily used to refer to the belief that instructional practices and technological supports are presently available to accommodate all students in the school and classroom they would otherwise attend if not disabled" (p. 8). The philosophical basis for full inclusion, in part, can be traced to the Regular Education Initiative.

Although still not many are totally inclusive schools, Stainback and Stainback (1992) identified some common characteristics:

1. Inclusive schools are grounded in the philosophy that all children belong in the mainstream of school community life.
2. The rules of an inclusive classroom reflect the philosophy of fair and equal treatment among all students as well as other school and community members.
3. Teachers in inclusive classrooms adjust and/or expand their general education curriculum as required to meet each student's needs.
4. These schools accept all students within the given neighborhood's school. In this way a natural proportion of handicapped students attend school in their age-appropriate, neighborhood school.
5. Inclusive schools focus on providing assistance, specialized support, and services to all students within the regular classroom.
6. These schools adapt, modify, and expand the curriculum by differentiating objectives within the regular classroom.

7. Inclusive schools foster interdependence and natural support networks among staff and students through cooperation and collaboration and by deemphasizing completion.
8. When a student requires expert assistance from outside the classroom, the classroom support system and curriculum are adapted to assist not only the needs of one student, but also other student who could benefit from similar supports.
9. Teachers and other staff personnel are empowered to make decisions on how the combined special education and regular education resources, in terms of money, personnel, curriculum, and instructional procedures, will be utilized to meet the needs of the students within the school.
10. Educators in inclusive schools and classroom are flexible and receptive to change when deemed necessary. (pp. 7–11)

According to Snell (1991), the three most important and reciprocal benefits from inclusion are "(a) the development of social skills across all age groups, (b) the improvements in the attitudes that nondisabled peers have for their peers with disabilities, and the (c) the development of positive relationships and friendships between peers as a result of integration" (1996, p. 9).

Critics of inclusive schools question how general education can respond appropriately to the needs of all social education students when it has such obvious difficulty accommodating the divergent student population that already exists (Fuchs & Fuchs, 1994). Many opponents believe that special education students will not get enough attention in the regular classroom, while others feel that the regular education student will suffer because pupils with special needs will require the majority of the classroom teacher's time (Stoler, 1992). The inclusionist vision of restructured schooling that deemphasizes the standard curriculum and advocates a process approach to education is in direct contrast to what is currently being written and supported by many reformers, policy makers, and educators (Fuchs & Fuchs, 1994).

When disabled students are integrated into general education classrooms, a major concern that emerges is the potential impact of the attitudes of regular classroom teachers toward these students (Garvar-Pinhas & Schmelkin, 1989). The attitudes and behaviors of educators toward any individual student can either enable the pupil to progress intellectually, socially, and emotionally, or can inhibit the child's opportunities for learning and growth.

Since a teacher's positive attitude toward a disabled child may facilitate the child's functioning and a negative attitude can magnify difficulties, the identification of teacher attitude is particularly crucial to the integration process (Choate, 1993). Because teachers' responses toward disabled students reflect their attitudes, building principals must be aware of the attitudes regular education teachers possess concerning the integration of disabled students. Without considering these attitudes and expectations, administrative decisions will result in inappropriate placement and poorly implemented programs.

Any discussion of inclusive practices must consider the effect on student achievement (Yell et al., 2006). That is to say, if students with disabilities in an inclusive setting do not adequately progress in their learning, then inclusion is not in their best interest. Simultaneously, inclusive practices should not interfere with the achievement of other students. Generally, academic outcomes in inclusive schools have been found to be positive for students (Hang & Rabren, 2009; Idol, 2006).

In a statewide study, researchers found that students with disabilities who spent more time in general education passed eighth-grade assessment at a higher rate than similar students with disabilities who were educated in special education settings. Students educated in general education settings also graduated at a higher rate from high school with a standard diploma (Luster & Durrett, 2003). Another statewide study found that school districts reporting the greatest achievement gains for students with disabilities focused on educating student with nondisabled peers so that all had access to the same core curriculum (Silverman, Hazelwood, & Cronin, 2009).

The perceptions of teachers and administrators regarding inclusive practices can be represented along a continuum (DeSimone & Parmar, 2006; Pavari & Monda-Amaya, 2001; Rea, McLaughlin, & Walther-Thomas, 2002). In some studies, general education teachers in elementary, middle, and high schools are found to believe strongly in inclusive practices based on high standards for students (King & Youngs, 2003; McLeskey et al., 2001). Teachers who support inclusive practices report making instructional accommodations to facilitate student learning and feeling positive about their work with students with disabilities (Clayton, Burdge, Denham, Kleinert, & Kearns, 2006).

Also, some teachers' perceptions of inclusive practices are more ambivalent (Kozik, Cooney, Vinciguerra, Gradel, & Black, 2009). They recognize the value of inclusive practices but are uncertain about implementation. In a study of mathematics (DeSimone & Parmar, 2006), the educators indicated that they had to learn enough about students with disabilities to adequately address their needs. Among the items frequently mentioned are a commitment to inclusive practices and knowledge of effective instructional strategies (Stanovich & Jordan, 2002). In addition, principals' support of inclusive practices is essential because principals are responsible for keeping the vision focused, fostering among staff an understanding of inclusion and nurturing the development of the skills and practices needed to implement these practices (Horrocks, White, & Roberts, 2008; Salisbury & McGregor, 2002).

Where students receive their educational services is guided by the principle of least restrictive environment (LRE), the setting in which they can succeed that is most likely the setting for other students. In today's schools, the LRE for most students is general education for more than 80 percent of the school day. The emphasis now is on designing a system of support in general education settings according to the Individuals with Disability Education Act (IDEA) continuum of placements, now referred to as the educational environment that must exist for student with disabilities.

In some ways, the various positive and negative influences on practices are like puzzle pieces. In today's schools some of the pieces may be missing and others difficult to fit into place; yet others may be readily addressed and fit easily into the larger picture. One way to put the puzzle together is to learn to teach in a way that is responsive to a wide range of student needs (Sobel & Taylor, 2006; Zascavage & Winterman, 2009).

The Educational Leadership Constituents Council's Standards for Advanced Programs in Educational Leadership strongly endorse the responsibility of school leaders to ensure the success of every student. The standards recognize that school leaders must ground their work in improving teaching and learning in their schools and must advocate for all students in their schools. According to McLaughlin (2012), the principal must provide the vision for effective special education, and they must also create and sustain an organization that respects all students, families, teachers, and staff, and foster collective responsibility.

GENERAL EDUCATION: INCLUSION OR CONTINUUM?

Special education presents one of the major challenges facing school leaders. Today, schools must provide students with disabilities appropriate access to the general curriculum and effective instructional support. Student progress must be monitored closely and demonstrated through participations in assessment efforts. Research suggests that the principal's role is pivotal in the special education process; however, few school leaders are well prepared for this responsibility.

Research has demonstrated that principals who focus on instructional issues demonstrate administrative support for special education, provide high-quality professional development for teachers, and produce enhanced outcomes for students with disabilities and for others at risk for school failure (Benz, Lindstrom, & Yovanoff, 2000; Gersten, Keating, Yovanoff, & Hamiss, 2001; Keams, Kleinert, & Clayton, 1998; Klinger et al., 2001). Thus, the extent of administrative support affects the extent to which teachers and specialists develop and implement interventions designed to improve student performance (Embrich, 2012; Noell & Witt, 1999).

Given the complexity of the principal's role, rising expectations for both student and professional performance, and increased accountability and public scrutiny, it is not surprising that fewer teacher leaders are choosing career paths that result in administrative positions (Barker, 1994; DiPaola & Tschannen-Moran, 2006; ERS, 2000; U.S. Bureau of Labor Statistics [USBLS], 2000–2001, 1996–1997). The shortage of qualified principals impacts the caliber of leadership in schools. It is difficult for individuals with little or no experience in schools to understand and appreciate the diverse needs of learners.

Even those with prior school experience who have little formal preparation for the role of principal rarely have adequate understanding of how to plan, coordinate, and deliver services to meet the needs of students with disabilities. The Council for Exceptional Children (CEC, 2001) argues that the principal's role is pivotal in the improvement of educational opportunities of students with disabilities and other learners at risk. If students with disabilities are to be served, principals must be stewards and coached in the development of a school culture of inclusiveness (Burello & Lashley, 2000; NASBE, 1992; NCD, 1995; NRC, 1997; NSDC, 2001).

In the public education system, special and general education structures began as conceptually and administratively separate entities. Central office or district directors administered educational programs for the disabled. Building principals were not directly involved in these students' educational lives (Whittier & Hewitt, 1993). Over the past twenty-five years, however, state and federal legislation and public attitudes have wrought radical changes related to the perceived and actual role of disabled individuals within society, particularly in educational provisions (Elliott & Riddle 1992; Trump & Hange, 1996).

Recently, there has been a much stronger commitment to educating all children with special needs in regular schools including those with severe learning disabilities (Trump & Hange, 1996). The instruction of students with disabilities is no longer associated with separate, "pull out" programs; instead, students with disabilities are presently being taught in regular classrooms with their non-disabled peers (Choate, 1993).

The major support for placement of individuals with disabilities into integrated settings derives from the Education for All Handicapped Children Act (1965), now known as the Individuals with Disabilities Education Act (IDEA) (Yell, 1995). This act set the stage for the regular classroom placement of students with disabilities and prompted significant changes in our system of public education. As public schools move toward the integration of disabled students into general education classrooms, the professional roles and responsibilities of general education teachers and principals are being redefined (Fritz & Miller, 1995).

General education teachers are an important component of the successful implementation of the integration process (Choates, 1989; Lombardi, 1994). The leadership of the principal is also critical to successful educational programming for children with disabilities (Beninghof & Singer, 1995). The school administrator should be extensively involved in decisions about the placement of students with disabilities since she or he is in a key position to ensure that all pupils with disabilities participate in academic and extracurricular programs so that these students have the opportunity to interact with nondisabled peers (Goor, Schwenn, & Boyer, 1997).

The principal is the instructional leader for all educational services for all students within the school, including special education programs (Van Hom, Burello, & DeClue, 1992). Certain attributes of effective leaders are essential to accomplishing educational environments and practices that help lead to success for all student. Beninghof and Singer (1995) indicate that leaders should be:

a. Driven by sound principles and beliefs;
b. Guided by a vision for the future;
c. Committed to empowering others to achieve greatness in students and schools through the management of human, material, and fiscal resources; and
d. Dedicated to leadership by example or "walking the talk." (p. 12)

The effective school administrator demonstrates an understanding of the needs of all students and the relation of these needs to the overall success of the school program (Sage & Burello, 1994). The principal should be able to implement required programs and to help with the strategies and resources that will address the wide range of student abilities in the classroom. It is essential that the principal identify and articulate a philosophy that reflects the following assumptions, according to Villa and Thousand (1996):

a. All children can learn;
b. All children have the right to be educated with their peers in appropriate heterogeneous classrooms in their local schools; and
c. It is the responsibility of the school system to meet the diverse educational and psychological needs of all students. (p. 7)

Effective principals realize that an active involvement with students and staff will result in related changes in classroom instruction (Campbell & Shaw, 1993). Teachers and principals, therefore, must work together closely if schools are to be successful. It is important that teachers be actively involved, have the ability to influence, and be given the responsibility in many instances to make decisions related to learning (Ambrosie, 1989).

The most recent debate in special education is focused on the degree to which full integration of all disabled students can be achieved through supporting a general education classroom environment rather than through a continuum of separate education environment. In 1986, Madeline Will of the U.S. Department of Education proposed the regular education initiative (REI), a plan unifying general and special education (OSERS, 1986). This initiative advocates that the general education system of public school assume responsibility for all students including those with disabilities. The federal Office of Special Education and Rehabilitative Services (OSERS) defines the integration of disabled student as:

1. Educating all disabled student children in regular school regardless of the degree or severity of their disabling conditions.
2. Providing special services with regular schools.
3. Supporting regular teachers and administrators.
4. Having students with disabilities follow the same schedules as nondisabled students.
5. Involving disabled students in as many academic classes and extracurricular activities as possible, including music, art, gym, field trips, assemblies, and graduation exercises.
6. Arranging for disabled students to use the school cafeteria, library, playground, and other facilities at the same time as students.
7. Encouraging helper buddy relationships between nondisabled and disabled students.
8. Arranging for disabled students to receive their education in regular community environments when appropriate.
9. Teaching all children to understand and accept human differences.
10. Taking parents' concerns seriously.
11. Providing an appropriate individualized education program. (pp. 6–7).

Proponents of the REI question the quality and value of special classes and pull-out programs for students with mild academic handicaps, including those children who are labeled learning disabled (LD), educable mentally retarded (EMR), or emotionally disturbed (ED). These advocates indicate that service provision outside the regular classroom had led to discontinuity in instruction and reduction of curricular options for students with exceptionalities, and other segregated programs included lower self-esteem for students with disabilities than for nondisabled peers (Rogers & Saklofske, 1985); less than adequate social skills (Madden & Slavin, 1983); and lack of preparation for adulthood, manifested by a high rate of unemployment among people with exceptionalities. REI supporters want a fundamentally restructured mainstream adjusted to the needs of each child. Such a solution, they believe, would lead to a better education for all children at a lower cost (Byrnes, 1990).

Providing support for the REI is the heightening concern that too many students are being labeled as disabled. Kauffman, Gerber, and Semmel (1988), cite the following reasons

a. few educators can argue against such reasons underlying the regular education initiative as the need to work toward better integration and coordination of services;
b. the desire to seek effective and economical methods of servicing students with learning and behavior problems;
c. the need to place student with their nondisabled peers;
d. the need to implement research that has suggested guidelines for effective schools and instruction;
e. the idea that special education should be for those students who need the most specialized and extensive services;
f. the belief that most good teaching practices are appropriate for many student regardless of their handicapping condition;
g. the fact that some students fail because of the inadequacy of teachers of regular classes;
h. the importance of a continuum of services ranging from full-time placement in the regular classroom to institutionalization; and
i. the difficulty of accurately identifying and assessing persons with disabilities (pp. 6–11).

As with most calls for reform, the REI met with opposition (Virginia Department of Education, 1993). Although critics of the regular education initiative also see problems with the current education system, they do not believe that the evidence is sufficient to warrant a major restructuring (Byrnes, 1990). REI opponents are fearful that the rights of students with disabilities would be jeopardized if existing categorical placements were modified or eliminated.

A major concern is that students who need special education services many not receive them in the regular education classroom (Kauffman, 1989). Another problem is that many general education teachers are not willing to accept the shared responsibility for educating disabled students since they lack the essential training. These teachers are already attempting to meet the needs of a diverse group of learners who make up the general education classroom.

The Jeffersonian Compact, a statement resulting from former President George H. W. Bush's Summit on Education, strongly encouraged the need for flexibility in using federal funds and encouraged the commitment to restructuring the schools to include decentralization of authority or school-based management (U.S. Department of Education, 1991). One recommendation that was made for the use of federal funds was the use of waivers to permit students qualifying for special education to return to regular classes with extra support.

The compact indicated that decentralization would mean greater choice for parents and students, greater authority for and accountability by teachers and principals, and instructional programs designed for all students to accomplish work skills (U.S. Department of Education, 1991). The results of the summit provide support for the belief that all students, regardless of their disabilities, belong in their neighborhood school and the principal should organize the program to meet the diverse and individualized needs of all children.

Currently, the job of a school leader has been transformed by extraordinary economic, demographic, technological, and global change. As our country makes the transition from an industrial to a global, information-based economy, everything around us is in flux—things as fundamental as what we do for a living, how we shop and communicate, where we live, and what our country's relationship is with the rest of the world (Levine, 2005).

In one way or another, every American citizen and all social institutions in the U.S. have been shaken by these sweeping changes, and the schools are no exception. Education has been turned into one of the most powerful engines driving our economy. To be competitive in a global marketplace, the United States now requires a more educated population. To be employable in an information society, our children need more advanced skills and knowledge than required in the past. The states have responded to these realities by raising standards for school promotion and graduation, mandating student testing, and demanding school accountability.

One major emphasis in the educational arena in the early twenty-first century has been the continuing demand for greater accountability to increase student performance. National and state expectations require schools to ensure that all students achieve mastery of curriculum objectives and local schools focus on implementing those requirements to the best of their ability. As a result, leading instructional efforts in a school has evolved into a primary role for school principals.

To meet the challenges associated with national and state expectations, principals must focus on teaching and learning—especially in terms of measurable student progress—to a greater degree than heretofore. Consequently, today's principals concentrate on building a vision for their schools, sharing leadership with teachers, and influencing schools to operate as learning communities. Accomplishing these essential school improvement efforts requires gathering and assessing data to determine needs and monitoring instruction and curriculum to determine if the identified needs are addressed.

According to McLaughlin (2012), too often, under the various state-developed standards and assessments, accommodations for students with disabilities—a heterogeneous group with varied characteristics and needs—have not been adequately addressed or have been ignored. The Common Core State Standards (CCSS) initiative provides a historic opportunity to improve access to rigorous academic content standards for students with disabilities. However, implementation of CCSS must begin with the characteristics of these students clearly in mind. Because no single method or approach provides all students with access to the Common Core, the two most important areas that need to be addressed in implementation are instruction and assessment.

Margaret Pratt, principal in a suburban elementary school in New York State's Putnam County, was an educator for fifteen years and a principal for seven years in the same district. She states:

> Challenges exist in the day-to-day life of a principal in elementary schools today. I have been the leader of my school for seven years. There was a time when I would have set goals not set by the state. I would have met state mandates through collaboration with my teachers and staff and would work with my parent groups to design the best programs to meet my students' needs. The challenge today is the inability to be autonomous and make decisions that are community based for your school. One daunting challenge is meeting the artificial expectations that are thrust upon us as leaders and that are converse to the expertise and experience held by educators in schools. How can I lead through a shared vision, set curriculum, and embrace best practices when I cannot make those decisions within the current state of education, which are accountability based—not by my metrics, that are test based, but not by teacher-created tests that relate to authentic student learning, and set standards when now we all have to reach college and career readiness standards that are not researched based? This current reality is wearily approached every day by principals all over the nation, state, and county. (Pratt, 2011)

Principals are central to enabling teachers to understand how to better address the learning needs of students. A key factor in creating better instruction is providing opportunities for general and special education teachers to share knowledge about evidence-based practices or interventions, as well as how to apply these to instruction in the Common Core State Standards (McLaughlin, 2012).

However, in addition to the state assessments, schools must put together an assessment system that can monitor student progress. Principals need to develop systems that build on continuous monitoring of student progress to augment the end-of-year snapshot measurement approach. These include curriculum-based measures, such as reading fluency probes, as well as performance-based tasks that can be measured across classrooms with common rubrics. Teachers, both general and special educators, should have time to examine and discuss student work and identify exemplary performances, as well as those areas where students are faltering.

The principal's most significant challenge is in preparing and further developing the knowledge and skills of not only special educators but all teachers and related service personnel who are sharing the instructional responsibilities for students.

The principal must foster a collective responsibility for the achievement of students with disabilities and help teachers define their role in providing access to the standards. If teachers do not deeply understand the standards, they are unable to design supports and accommodations or instruction that will provide a potential for mastery. If teachers are not familiar with various means of assessing progress, they won't know how instruction needs to be adjusted to increase the probability of mastery. If teachers are not deeply knowledgeable about the various effective strategies for teaching reading and math that have been shown to produce results, the likelihood that any student with a disability will be able to navigate these standards in English language arts and math is slim.

Principals need to understand the importance of creating supportive social and behavioral environments that will enable all students to access and achieve success in the general curriculum. Principals support instructional activities and programs by modeling expected behaviors, participating in staff development (as noted earlier), and consistently prioritizing instructional concerns on a day-to-day basis. They strive to protect instructional time by removing issues that would detract teachers from their instructional responsibilities (Marzano et al., 2005). Moreover, principals in effective schools are involved in instruction and work to provide resources that keep teachers focused on student achievement. They are knowledgeable about curriculum and instruction and promote teacher reflection about instruction and its effect on student achievement (Cotton, 2003). The most important challenge is to ensure educators are prepared to achieve that purpose.

The demands that accompany high-stakes testing compel principals to guide their schools to learn from their results and experiences. Doing so will lead to coherence within a school and offer better opportunities to sustain results. Additionally, continuous improvement requires principals to examine data and find means to address inconsistencies with expected results (Fullan, 1991).

Useful and properly mined data can inform staff about the gaps between desired outcomes and the reality of the results. Furthermore, this knowledge should result in changes in practice. Encouraging staff to collect, analyze, and determine appropriate actions based on the results should be a collective enterprise. When staff members assume an active role in the data analysis process, it promotes solutions and actions for improving results (Zmuda et al., 2004), and facilitating the active involvement of all staff in information gathering and analysis is the prerogative of the principal.

What follows is a summary of key indicators of the role of effective principals and gathering and using data in their schools:

- Effective school leaders skillfully gather data and use it to determine school effectiveness (Leithwood & Riehl, 2003).

- Continuous improvement requires an examination of the data (Fullan, 2005).
- Greater results are achieved when principals encourage school staff to actively analyze data for improving results (Zmuda et al., 2004).

Nothing in the principal's role is more important for ensuring successful student learning than effective instructional leadership. School principals who focus on a vision for their schools nurture the leadership capabilities of their teachers. Additionally, if their schools are moving in the right direction, they model effective leading and learning. Combining these efforts with using data appropriately, as well as monitoring what takes place at the classroom level, will increase the likelihood that schools will achieve their goals for all students learning.

REFERENCES

Ambrosie, C. (1989). *Theories and Practices for Differentiated Education for Gifted and Talented.* Pacific University, Forrest Grove, Oregon, USA.

Barker, Bruce O., & Hall, Robert F. (1994). A national survey of distance education use in rural school districts of 300 students or less — Paper presented at the Annual Conference of the National Rural Education Association (85th, Bur lington, VT, October 14-17, 1993). RIE, 16;1.

Beninghof, A., & Singer, A. T. (1995). Inclusion for inclusion: The school administrative guide. Longmont, CO: Sopris West.

Benz, M., Lindstrom, L., & Yovanoff, P. (2000). *Sustaining Secondary Transition Programs in Local Schools. Remedial* & Special Education. January/February 2004, 25:39–50.

Burello, L. C., Schrup, M. G., & Barnett, B. G. (1988). *The principal as the special education instructional leader.* Presentation at the annual Convention of the Council for Exceptional Children. Washington, DC.

Burello, L. C., Lashley, C. L., & Beatty, Edith E. (2001). *Educating All Students Together: How Leaders Create Unified Systems.* Thousand Oaks, CA: Corwin Press.

Byrnes, M. (1990). The regular education initiative debate: A review from the field. *Exceptional Children, 56*(4), 71–77.

Campbell, P., & Shaw, S. F. (1993). A process for systematic change: Planning for special education in the 21st century. *CASE in Point, 7*(2) 47–52.

Choate, J. (1993). *Successful mainstreaming: Proven ways to detect and correct special needs.* Boston: Allyn & Bacon.

Choates, R. D. (1989). *Successful Mainstreaming - Proven Ways to Detect and Correct Special Needs.* Boston: Allyn & Bacon.

Clayton, J., Burdge, M., Denham, A., Kleinert, H., & Kearns, J. (2006). A four-step process for accessing the general curriculum for students with significant cognitive disabilities. *Teaching Exceptional Children, 38*(5), 20–27.

Cotton, K. (2003). Principals and Student Achievement: What the Research Says. Association for Supervision & Curriculum Development.

Council for Exceptional Children. (2001). *Bright futures for exceptional learners: An agenda to achieve duality conditions for teaching and learning.* Arlington, VA: Author.

DeSimone, J. R., and Parmar, R. S. (2006). Issues and Challenges for Middle School Mathematics Teachers in Inclusion Classrooms. School Science and Mathematics, 106: 338–348. doi: 10.1111/j.1949-8594.2006.tb17754.x.

DiPaola, M. F., & Tschannen-Moran, M. (2006). Bridging or buffering? The impact of schools' adaptive strategies on student achievement. *Journal of Educational Administration, 43*(1), 60–71.

Elliott, B., & Riddle, M. (1992). *An effective interface between regular and special education: A synopsis of issues and successful practices.* Bloomington, Indiana: Council of Administrators in Special Education Inc.

Emrich, S. M., Wilson, K. E., Stergiopoulos, E., & Ferber, S. (2012). In and out of consciousness: sustained electrophysiological activity reflects individual differences in perceptual awareness. *Psychonomic Bulletin & Review, 19*(3), 429–435.

ERS. (2000). *The principal, keystone of a high-achieving school: Attracting and keeping the leaders we need.* Washington, DC: National Association of Elementary School Principals and National Association of Secondary School Principals.

Fritz & Miller. (1995). School climate, sense of efficacy and Israeli teachers' attitudes toward inclusion of students with special needs. *Education, Citizenship and Social Justice* July 2006 1:157–174.

Fuchs, D., & Fuchs, L. S. (1994). Inclusive Schools Movement and the Radicalization of Special Education Reform. *Exceptional Children, 60,* 294–309.

Fullan, M. (1991). *The New Meaning of Educational Change.* New York: Teachers College Press.

Garvar-Pinhas, A., & Schmelkin, L. P. (1989). Administrators' and Teaches Attitudes Toward Mainstreaming. *Remedial and Special Education, 10,* 38–43.

Goor, M., Schwenn, J. O., & Boyer, L. (1997). Preparing Principals for Leadership in Special Education. *Intervention in School and Clinic, 32*(3), 133–141.

Gratz, D. (2009). Special Topic—The Problem with Performance Pay. *Educational Leadership,* Multiple Measures Pages 76–79.

Hang & Rabren. (2009). An Examination of Co-Teaching. Perspectives and Efficacy Indicators. *The Journal of Remedial and Special Education, 30*(5), 259-268.

Horrocks, J., White, G., & Roberts, L. (2008). Principals' Attitudes Regarding Inclusion of Children with Autism in Pennsylvania Public Schools. *Journal of Autism and Developmental Disorders,* Volume 38, Issue 8, 1462–1473.

Idol, L. (2006). A study of four schools: Inclusion of students with disabilities in four secondary schools. Austin, TX: Austin Independent School District, Office of Program Evaluation.

Individuals with Disabilities Education Act, 1400 34 C.F.R. Part 300 (1997).

Individuals with Disabilities Education Act Amendments of 1997, 20 U.S.S.

Individualized Education Program (IEP) (2008). U. S. Department of Education, Office of Special Education Programs.

Kauffman, J. M. (1989). The regular education initiative as Reagan–Bush education policy: A trickle-down theory of education of the hard-to-teach. *Journal of Special Education, 23,* 256–278.

Kauffman, J. M., Gerber, M. M., & Semmel, M. I. (1988). Arguable assumptions underlying the Regular Education Initiative, *Journal of learning Disabilities, 21,* 6-11.

King, K. P. (2003). *Keeping pace with technology: Educational technology that transforms – Volume Two: The challenge and promise for educators in higher education.* Cresskill, NJ: Hampton Press.

Kozik, P. L., Cooney, B., Vinciguerra, S., Gradel, K., & Black, J. (2009). Promoting inclusion in secondary schools through appreciative inquiry. *American Secondary Education, 38*(1), 77-91.

Leithwood, K. A., & Riehl, C. (2003). *What we know about successful school leadership.* Philadelphia, PA: Laboratory for Student Success, Temple University.

Levine, A. (2005). *Educating School Leaders.* New York: The Education School Project.

Lombardi, T. (1994). Responsible Inclusion of Students with Disabilities. Bloomington, Indiana Phi Delta Kappa Educational Foundation.

Luster, J. N., & Durrett, J. (2003). *Does educational placement matter in the performance of students with disabilities?* Paper presented at the meeting of the Mid-South Educational Research Association, Biloxi, MS.

Madden, N., & Slavin, R. (1983). Mainstreaming Students with Mild Handicaps: Academic and Social Outcomes. *Review of Educational Research*, Winter 1983, 53, 519–569.

Marzano, R. J., Waters, T., & McNulty, B. A. (2005). School leadership that works: From research to results. Alexandria, VA: Association for Supervision and Curriculum Development (ASCD).

McLaughlin, M. (2009). *What Every Principal Needs to Know About Special Education.* New York: Corwin-Sage.

McLaughlin, M. (2012). Six principles for principals to consider in implementing CCSS for students with disabilities. National Association of Elementary Principals (NAESP).

National Center for Education Statistics. (2001). The Condition of Education 2001.

National Council of Disabilities [NCD]. (1995). *Improving the implementation of the Individuals with Disabilities Act: Making Schools work for all of America's children.* Washington, DC: Author.

National Research Council [NRC]. (1997). *Educating one and all: students with disabilities and standards-based reform.* Washington, DC: National Academy Press.

National Staff Development Council [NSDC]. (2001). *Learning to lead, leading to learn: Improving school quality through principal professional development.* Oxford: OH, Author.

Noell, G. H., & Witt, J. C. (1999). When does consultation lead to intervention implementation? *Journal of Special Education, 33,* 29–41.

Noell, G. H., & Witt, J. C. (1999). Toward a behavior analytic approach to consultation. In T. S. Watson & F. M. Gersham (eds). *Handbook of child behavior therapy.* New York: Plenum.

OSERS. (1986). Office of Special Education and Rehabilitation Services: Gallaudet University: Education of the Deaf Act 1986 (EDA).

Pavari, S., & Monda-Amaya, L. (2001). Social support in inclusive schools: Student and teacher perspectives. *Exceptional Children, 67,* 391–411.

Rea, P. J., McLaughlin, V. L., & Walther-Thomas, C. (2002). Outcomes for students with learning disabilities in inclusive and pullout programs. *Exceptional Children, 68,* 203–223.

Rogers, C. R. (1994). *Freedom to Learn.* Columbus, OH: Merrill.

Rogers, J. H., & Saklofske, D. H. (1985). Self-Concepts, Locus of Control and Performance Expectations of Learning Disabled Children. *Journal of Learning Disabilities.*

Sage, D. D., & Burrello, L. C. (1994). *Leadership in educational reform: An administrator's guide to changes in special education.* Baltimore, MD: Paul H. Brookes.

Salisbury, C., & McGregor, G. (2002). The administrative climate and context of inclusive elementary schools. *Exceptional Children, 68*(2), 259–274.

Silverman, S, Hazelwood, C., & Cronin. P. (2009). Universal Education: Principles and Practices for Advancing Achievement of Students with Disabilities. Ohio Department of Education.

Snell, M. E. (1991). Schools are for all kids: The importance of integration for students with severe disabilities and their peers. In J. W. Lloyd, N. N. Singh & A. C. Repp (Eds). *The regular education initiative: Alternative perspectives on concepts, issues and models,* pp.133–149. Sycamore, IL: Sycamore.

Sobel, D. M., & Taylor, S. V. (2006). Blueprint for the responsive classroom. *Teaching Exceptional Children, 38*(5), 28–35.

Stainback, W., & Stainback, S. (1992). *Support networks for inclusive schooling: Interdependent Integrated Education.* Baltimore: Brookes Publishing Company.

Stanovich, P., & Jordan, A. (2002). Preparing general educators to teach in inclusive classrooms: some food for thought. *The Teacher Educator, 37*(3), 173–185.

Stoler, R. (1992). *Perceptions of Regular Education Teachers toward Inclusion of All Handicapped Students in Their Classrooms* The Clearing House - September/October 1992, 60–62. *School Journal, 98,* 221–238.

Trump, G. C., & Hange, J. E. (1996). Concerns about the effective strategies for inclusion: Focus group interview findings from Virginia teachers. Charleston, WV: Applachia Educational Lab . (ERIC Reproduction Services No. ED 397 577.

U.S. Department of Education. (2009). 28th Annual Report to Congress on the Implementation of the individuals with Disabilities Education Act. 2006, vol. 1. Washington, DC: U.S. Government Printing Office.

U.S. Department of Education, National Center for Education Statistics. (1997). *Digest of Education Statistics 1997*. Washington, DC.

Van Horn, G. P., Burrello, L., & DeClue, L. (1992). An instructional leadership framework: The principal role in special education. *The Leadership Review, 1*, 41–54.

Villa, R. A., Thousand, Meyers, & Nixon. (1996). Teacher and administrator perceptions of heterogeneous education. *Exceptional Children, 63*(1), 29.

Virginia Department of Education. (1993). *Regulations Governing Special Education Programs for Children with Disabilities in Virginia*, 8 VAC 20-80-10 et seq. 1993.

Yell, M. (1995). The Least Restrictive Environment: A Place or a Context? *Remedial and Special Education*, March 2000, 21: 70–78.

Yell, M. (2006). *The law and special education*. NJ: Prentice Hall.

Zascavage, V., & Winterman, K. G. (2009). What Middle School Educators Should Know About Assistive Technology and Universal Design for Learning. *Middle School Journal, 40*(4), 46–52.

Zmuda, A., Kuklis, R., & Kline, E. (2004). *Transforming schools: Creating a culture of continuous school improvement*. Alexandria, VA: Association for Supervision and Curriculum Development.

FOUR

Where Do We Begin?

Kathryn F. Accurso

Good teaching is more than picking up a bag of instructional tricks at the schoolroom door or learning to mimic the actions of another educator — even a very notable one. Good teachers are thinkers and problem solvers. They know when children aren't learning and can adjust instruction appropriately; they know how to work with parents to bring out the best in a child; they know that teams of professional educators can transform schools and expect to go about doing it (Imig, 1996, p. l4A).

The U.S. Congress passed the Education for All Handicapped Children Act, subsequently renamed the Individuals with Disabilities Education Improvement Act (IDEA), in 1975, reauthorized it in 1997, and followed it with the implementation of the No Child left Behind Act of 2001 (NCLB) (U.S. Department of Education, 2001), which included a mandate that students with disabilities be educated in the least restrictive environment (LRE). This policy has led the way for students with disabilities to be been placed in general education classrooms. Inclusion, the practice of including students with disabilities in general education classrooms, is quickly becoming the norm in education.

Although the Education of All Handicapped Children Act (1975) guarantees students with handicapping conditions a free and appropriate education in the least restrictive environment, few agree on what the "least restrictive environment" means.

The Individuals with Disabilities Education Act (IDEA) further provides that states must have in place procedures assuring that,

> to the maximum extent appropriate, children with disabilities, including children in public or private institutions or other care facilities, are educated with children who are not disabled, and that special classes,

separate schooling, or other removal of children with disabilities from the regular educational environment occurs only when the nature or severity of the disability is such that education in regular classes with the use of supplementary aids and services cannot be achieved satisfactorily. (np)

In recent years, the topic of inclusion has generated fear, confusion, and anxiety for teachers, parents, and administrators alike. It seems that it doesn't matter whether one is an opponent, supporter, or neutral onlooker of inclusion, there is much to discuss. Certainly, districts are responding to parents' concerns as well as state mandates calling for students to be educated in the LRE. However, we see a great deal to consider when districts make the commitment to accommodate students with disabilities in the general education classrooms. To complicate the issue further, several terms are used interchangeable but are in actuality quite different, when referring to placement of special needs students in different settings.

SELF-CONTAINED CLASSROOMS

A self-contained classroom is a setting made up of special needs students who would benefit from being in a structured classroom with fewer students than in a general education classroom. The teacher in the self-contained classroom has been trained to work with special needs students and is available to help each student make progress toward the goals on their individualized education plans (IEP). Self-contained classrooms often have a teaching assistant as well, meaning that the student-to-adult ratio is much lower than that in a general education classroom. Oftentimes, these students have music, art, gym, and lunch with the general education students but have their content area subject instruction in the self-contained classroom.

MAINSTREAMING

According to Rogers (1993), "mainstreaming has generally been used to refer to the selective placement of special education students in one or more 'regular' education classes. . . . [Mainstreaming generally assumes] that a student must 'earn' his or her opportunity to be mainstreamed through the ability to 'keep up with the work assigned by the teacher to the other students in the class'" (p. 1). In this situation the student may join the general education class for one or more content area subjects, such as math, social studies, science, or English language arts (ELA) and then return to a self-contained classroom for the remainder of his or her instruction.

INCLUSIVE CLASSROOMS

In the inclusive classroom, students with special needs and general education students work side by side in the same classroom. The students with disabilities are placed in age-appropriate classrooms in their home districts, according to individual abilities and needs, where they receive specialized instruction within the general education class. "The true essence of inclusion is based on the premise that all individuals with disabilities have a right to be included in naturally occurring settings and activities with their neighborhood peers, siblings, and friends" (Erwin, 1993, p. 3–4).

COTEACH CLASSROOMS

In a coteach classroom, a general education teacher and special education teacher work together in one classroom. Coteaching varies slightly from district to district, but all have the same premise: students with disabilities and general education students are placed in the same coteach class. Having two teachers allows for more individualized instruction, provides for various supports in the classroom, and allows the teachers to address the learning styles of all students.

TEACHER TRAINING

While more and more general educators are expected to accommodate students with special needs in their classrooms, few of these teachers feel that they have been provided with the staff development needed to meet this challenge.

Recently, a colleague was informed that he would be getting a new student who, until recently, had been in a self-contained classroom, and was now to be a full inclusion student in his classroom. Feeling that he needed more information as to how he could meet the needs of this student while addressing the needs of the remaining twenty-three students in his classroom, the teacher began to look for articles online. He showed me an article printed from a popular education website. The piece was titled, "Meeting the Needs of Special Needs Students in the Inclusion Classroom." Imagine my surprise as I read the article: "Students within the classroom frequently provide valuable support for teachers overseeing inclusion classrooms." The article went on to say that teachers have found that using nondisabled students in their classrooms has freed them up to work with the special needs students. The teachers have the "good" students work independently with the special needs students. Reportedly, this not only reduces stress but also allows the teacher more time to work with struggling students. While the benefits of peer tutoring have long been recognized, when it becomes the principal method of instruction, neither student's needs are being met appropriately. Unfortunately, this idea that the brighter students in the class can support the more needy students is just what is happening in many classrooms, and neither the special needs student nor the general education student are benefiting.

I'm reminded of a parent of a classified middle school student, who also had a fourth-grader. Lynn, the fourth-grader, was a bright, hardworking student—the kind who was always asking the teacher "what's next?" The fourth-grade teacher, Mrs. Lane, was overwhelmed when she learned early one November morning that she was getting a new student, John, classified as a special needs child. His parents had fought to have their son enrolled in a general education class. Mrs. Lane indicated that she didn't feel qualified to meet the needs of such a student in her classroom. With twenty-three other students, who also needed her time and attention, Mrs. Lane quickly realized she wasn't able to give John the support he needed to be successful.

A colleague suggested that she enlist the help of one of her more capable students, which she did. Soon Lynn was helping John with most of his daily assignments, checking his homework assignment pad, and making sure he had packed all the books that he would need to complete that night's homework. Quite a task for a fourth-grader!

At the end of the school year, Lynn's parents received a letter from Mrs. Lane, the classroom teacher, and the school principal, Mrs. Small, commending Lynn for helping the student with special needs. Of course, when Lynn's mother read the letter, she was so proud, sure that Lynn had taken this student under her wing because she understood his struggles, having seen her own brother struggle with school.

That night at the dinner table, Lynn's mother read the letter from the school to the family. The family praised Lynn for her selflessness, at which point Lynn began to cry. She explained that it was very stressful for her to be responsible for another student. She also told her parents that she found it difficult to get her work done because John had required so much help. John received the help he needed to assimilate in the classroom, but what about Lynn? Was her full potential maximized or compromised?

Better ways exist for teachers to support the needs of all students, those who are classified and those whose potential needs to be recognized, not ignored. Unfortunately, since many teachers leave their respective universities without much training in how to do this and with a focus on core curriculum and standardized testing, learning to maximize instruction is too often missed.

If we want our students to receive an education that will prepare them for *success*, then we must ensure that we are educating our teachers to move them in that direction. According to Miller (2009), it is well established that teacher quality is one of the most significant school influences on student achievement. Unfortunately, it is less clear how teacher education programs can prepare and recruit effective educators for every classroom. Lack of research, insufficient data-collection systems, and no definitive agreement as to the preparation candidates need have resulted in a long-standing debate about teacher education in our country. But policy makers, researchers, and practitioners alike are still seeking more effective reforms of the preparation teachers receive before they enter the classroom—something not happening as rapidly or extensively as needed.

Children and young adults (ages three to twenty-one) receiving special education services in public schools rose from 3.7 million students (about 5 percent of the total) in 1976 to about 6.7 million students (9 percent) in 2007 (U.S. Department of Education, 2009). One has only to look at the numbers to realize the need for general education and special education teachers to work together to meet the needs of all students. This translates into the gap in the teacher preparation programs. Each year teachers are required to teach to a group of students that they feel ill prepared to teach.

This fact is not an indication of the attitudes of the teacher or school system, but rather a reflection of the universities and colleges that are preparing our teachers for the classroom. Many teacher preparation programs barely skim the surface of the needs of special education students in the general education population. Only recently have universities and colleges begun to include special education training into their general education teacher preparation programs.

Efforts to effectively prepare teachers to work in inclusive classrooms require universities and colleges to rethink their traditional teacher preparation programs. Today, schools need teachers who are trained to meet the needs of a diverse classroom. If, as Blanton (1992) suggests "the goal of teacher preparation programs is to provide experiences that assist teacher candidates in transforming knowledge into personal knowledge structures that can be used in a flexible way during teaching, this change in preservice teacher education must extend beyond the classroom into quality fieldwork experiences as well" (pp. 87–96).

One promising approach to helping teachers more effectively serve all K–12 learners requires fundamental change in the nature of their preparation. A number of models of collaborative teacher education have been developed, including those termed integrated, unified, or merged. These new approaches to teacher education vary according to the degree of collaboration among faculty and the extent to which curricular components from general and special education programs are integrated through a process of collaborative program redesign (Blanton & Pugach, 2006).

Ann, a first-year teacher, was hired as one-half of a teaching team in a collaborative classroom. The other teacher in the classroom was Tom, a seasoned, certified special education teacher of fifteen years. This particular district had the two teachers in the classroom where they shared teaching duties for the morning. Although Ann will admit she relied heavily on Tom to help her with the special education students.

The class consisted of six classified students as well as sixteen general education students. After lunch, Tom left the room to work with another group of special education students. Ann was left to teach the class solo.

Ann said it didn't take her long to she realize she was in over her head. She was not prepared to meet the needs of the special education students in the classroom. She went on to say that her coursework in college rarely included information on how to teach special education students or even how to differentiate her lessons to meet the needs of the remaining students in the class. Ann still talks about that first year and how she almost left teaching. She says it wasn't because she was unhappy with teaching but because she felt unprepared for the job. She explained, "I felt I let the students down. . . . They looked to me to help them learn, and most mornings I was reading anything I could to help me learn how to teach them in a way that made sense to them."

Ann returned to school and received an advanced certification in special education. One can't help but think of the good teachers who actually did leave teaching because they were unprepared or the teachers who are still teaching in similar situations without the appropriate training. Neither situation leaves a feeling good about the state of our teacher preparation programs.

Good teachers are critical. The research is clear—the single most important thing that a school can provide to ensure the success of students is a skilled and knowledgeable teacher. Good teachers—those who know what to teach and how to teach it—produce successful students. But teachers who are underqualified or ill equipped do not produce successful students (Center for the Future of Teaching and Learning, 2000).

In looking at improving teacher preparation programs, we need to look at the institutions themselves, as well as the teacher educators. Possibly many teacher educators have not been in school classrooms for many years and do not have firsthand knowledge of inclusive classrooms. Although not a new concept in education, inclusive classrooms are becoming more frequent in today's society than they were just a few short years ago. Also a real possibility is that the teacher educator many not agree with the philosophy of mixing general education and special education students in the classroom. When responding to improving our teacher preparation programs, we may need to also look at providing support to our teacher educators and curriculum writers.

We see an increasing need for highly qualified teachers as described by the current legislation in No Child Left Behind (2002). Since this legislative mandate has been enforced, recent initiatives have signaled teacher education programs to examine performance standards in demonstrating preparation of effective teachers for diverse learners. With more than six million children receiving services of one kind or another, the call for teachers who are able to meet the needs of all K–12 students is crucial.

A GOOD FIT?

Several different placement options mean that a school may find appropriate placement for a student with special needs. Some parents prefer and advocate for inclusive placement, while others favor separate placement (Grove & Fisher, 1999). Many special needs students receive a wide range of support services at school. Parents fear inclusion because they do not want their child to lose these services. Daniel and King (1997) found that parents were more concerned about the degree to which their child's individual education plan actually addressed the needs of their children when the children were being educated in an inclusive setting, as opposed to a segregated setting. It may be difficult for parents to find schools with personnel who are sufficiently knowledgeable about inclusive educational goals to provide appropriate services to their children (Grove & Fisher, 1999).

Some parents who did not want their children educated in an inclusive setting reported that they felt the nature of their children's disability precluded them from being candidates for an inclusive classroom. Parents' fears also included the possibility of the classroom teacher not having the proper training. Class size, classroom management, as well as the teacher's knowledge of teaching to a variety of learning styles were also of grave concern to parents.

Parents were also quick to discuss their concerns regarding the focus on academics in a general education classroom, as opposed to life skills, which would be taught in a special education class. Parents of children with more severe disabilities wanted their children to have more time spent learning life skills that they thought would be more beneficial for them. These parents were also troubled to think that their children would not get the one-on-one attention they would receive in a special education classroom. They voiced concerns over how well their child would be accepted socially in a general education classroom. Parents also expressed their concerns about students with moderate to severe emotional disabilities being included in the classroom.

A good number of the parents recognized the importance of smaller class size and the additional benefits that come along with being in a special education class such as push-in services from speech and language specialist, occupational therapist, counseling, and teacher training.

These same parents wanted their child with a disability to attend the same school as the child's sibling(s).

What does an inclusive classroom look like from the inside? Typically, each special needs student has an IEP that outlines the students' learning goals for the year. Often these goals are not the same as those goals for the general education students in the classroom. The teacher has to find a way to implement the curriculum in such a way as to benefit all the students in the classroom. When the special needs student's needs require the material taught on a different level or taught in several different modalities, it is difficult enough for a teacher who has not had the proper training, but what about the students who have emotional issues and require more hands-on time from the teacher? What happens to the remainder of the students while the teacher is addressing the needs of the special education student?

Let's imagine, if we can, the student with a moderate to severe emotional disability that is placed in an inclusive classroom. Although this student has a different kind of disability, the disability is just as real as the other special education students, at times requiring a more specialized approach in the classroom. As stated previously, many times the classroom teacher is not equipped to deal with such needs. When a problem arises, the teacher must stop teaching to defuse the situation or to call for the support staff, such as the school social worker or psychologist. Not only does this take away from instructional time, but it also is distressing to the other students in the classroom. These students are not accustomed to such outbursts in the classroom. Long after the incident is over, the students are still affected by it.

The classroom should be a safe environment for all the students, a place where the students are free to explore, learn, and grow without worrying about emotional upheavals. In this situation, one might argue that an inclusive classroom is not the best setting for this particular student. Were this student in a more specialized class, one that better fit the needs of a student with a moderate to severe emotional disability, the teacher would be trained to deal with such issues, as would the classroom aide. Many times the support staff pushes into these classrooms to offer support to the students on a regular schedule in an effort to avoid such outbursts.

More than forty states have adopted the new Common Core State Standards, which have districts around the country rewriting curriculum to meet the more rigorous coursework. The Common Core Standards are designed to help make our students more college and career ready. What happens in the inclusion classroom when the special needs student requires more support than the teacher is able to give? The Common Core Standards are causing much stress for many, teachers and students alike. Because of the way the Common Core Standards were implemented, many students do not have the prerequisite skills necessary to learn the new information. This leaves the teacher trying to fill in the gaps for these students and teaching the prerequisite skills along with current skills.

In the inclusive classroom, the teacher may be required to give the special needs students more hands-on time to catch them up to the class, leaving the rest of the class without the support they so desperately need during this very trying time in education.

While the special education students have a right to be challenged to excel within the general education curriculum based on the Common Core State Standards, the general education students also have a right to the support they need in the classroom in order to be successful. With the mounting pressure of the new curriculum, more assessments, and teacher evaluations being tied to student progress, teachers are stretched thin trying to ensure that all students are engaged and supported; thus, few have the time necessary to teach the basics, let alone give extra time to those students who are having trouble learning the curriculum in the time allotted.

MOVING FORWARD

In an effort to provide special education students with an appropriate education in the least restrictive environment, districts have tried different approaches with various degrees of success. Most recently, districts are looking to provide these students meaningful access to general education classes. Inclusive classrooms, where students with special needs and general education students work side by side in the same classroom, is one way districts have tried to do this. One issue that schools have had with inclusive classes is that the not all general education teachers have the proper training to work with special needs students. Managing a class of general and special education students requires great skill and knowledge to ensure that all the student's needs are being met. Without the proper training, general education teachers feel they are unprepared for this assignment.

Another way districts are looking to provide special needs students with the appropriate education is to provide these students with coteach classes. In a coteach classroom, a general education teacher and special education teacher work together in one classroom, with the purpose of delivering high-quality instruction to diverse classroom groups. Students with disabilities and general education students are placed in the same coteach class. Having two teachers allows for more individualized instruction, provides for various supports in the classroom, and allows the teachers to address the learning styles of all students. The goal is to maintain the standard for most learners while making accommodations for those students who need them. Coteach classes have the advantage of having a special education teacher on board, along with a general education teacher, as opposed to an inclusion class where there is only a general education teacher, who may or may not have had training in working with special education students.

One perceived benefit for children without disabilities was the positive role model coteaching provides when coteachers demonstrate successful collaboration. In addition, participants observed greater cooperation between students in cotaught inclusive classrooms. Some students also reported that when coteachers drift around the class assisting whoever needs help, the attention paid to all students increases, not just to students with special education needs (Scruggs, Mastropieri, & McDuffie, 2007).

Grade-level teams meet regularly to discuss curriculum and problem solve about students. Special education specialists along with other service providers frequently join the team to help with adapting the curriculum and create interventions to meet the diverse needs of the students in the coteach class. Having ongoing communication is key to a successful coteach program.

District and building level administrative support is essential to creating a supportive environment for a successful coteach class. As with any change, creating a coteach program in a school will have its challenges. However, having the administrator's support ensures that the teachers have the necessary resources needed to be successful, such as professional development and time to collaborate.

Trying to implement any new instructional technique into a school community can be challenging. Coteaching can be successful when it is implemented consistently, becomes part of the district mission statement, is supported by administrators through professional development, and uses the date collected from the classroom to guide its practice.

REFERENCES

Blanton, L. P. (1992). Pre-service education: Essential knowledge for the effective special educator. *Teacher Education and special education, 15*(2), 87–96.

Blanton, L. P., & Pugach, M. C. (2006). Collaborative programs in general and special education: An action guide for higher eduction and policymakers. Washington, DC: Council of Chief State School Officers. Center for Improving Teacher Quality.

The Center for the Future of Teaching & Learning at West Ed. http://www.cftl.org.

Daniel, L. G., & King, D. A. (1997). Impact of inclusion education on academic achievement, student behavior and self-esteem, and parental attitudes. *Journal of Educational Research, 91*(2), 67–80.

Danielson, L., & Bellamy, T. (1989). State variation in placement of children with handicaps in segregated environments. *Exceptional Children, 55*, 448–455.

Education Corner. Meeting the Needs of Special Needs Students in the Inclusion Classroom. http://www.educationcorner.com/special-needs-inclusion-classroom.html.

Erwin, E. J. (1993). The philosophy and status of inclusion. *Envision: A publication of the Lighthouse National Center for Vision and Child Development, 1*(Winter), 3–4.

Grove, K. A. & Fisher, D. (1999). Entrepreneurs of meaning: Parents and the process of inclusive education. *Remedial and Special Education, 20*(4), 208–215, 256.

Individuals with Disability Education Act Amendments of 1997 [IDEA]. (1997). Retrieved from http://thomas.loc.gov/home/thomas.php.

Imig, D. G. (1996, June 7). Not everyone can teach. *USA Today*, p. 14A.

Miller, M. (2009). Teaching for a new world: Preparing high school educators to deliver college- and career-ready instruction. *Alliance for Excellent Education.* http://eric.ed.gov/?id=ED507351.

Rogers, J. (1993, May). The inclusion revolution. *Phi Delta Kappan Research Bulletin* (11), 1–6.

Scruggs, T. A., Mastropieri, M. A., & McDuffie, K. A. (2007). Co-teaching in inclusive classrooms: A metasynthesis of qualitative research. *Exceptional Children, 73*(4), 392–416.

U.S. Department of Education. (2001). Executive summary of No Child Left Behind.

U.S. Department of Education, Institute for Education Sciences, National Center for Education Statistics. (2009). *The condition of education 2009* (NCES 2009081). Washington, DC: U.S. Government Printing Office.

FIVE

Teacher Preparation

Janet D. Mulvey

> To keep America competitive, and to make the American dream of
> equal educational opportunity a reality, we need to recruit, reward,
> train, learn from, and honor a new generation of talented teachers. But
> the bar must be raised for successful teacher preparation programs
> because we ask much more of teachers today than even a decade ago.
> Today teachers are asked to achieve significant academic growth for all
> students at the same time that they instruct students with ever-more
> diverse needs. Teaching has never been more difficult, it has never
> been more important, and the desperate need for more student success
> has never been so urgent. Are we adequately preparing future teachers
> to win this critical battle?
> —U.S. Secretary of Education Arne Duncan (2009)

Teacher training for the twenty-first century has proposed several core
standards for global competency and competitiveness. As already states
in chapter 1, the standards set by the American Association of Colleges
for Teacher Training clearly states the need for these skills but does not
specify what the skills are. Core principles, as outlined, assures teacher
knowledge in promoting inquiry, child development, diversity, critical
thinking and performance skills, learning environments, communication
skills, assessment and collaborative environments. The question is how
do we accomplish this in the current climate of testing and inclusion?

Proficiency and the ability to implement the above principles call for
college programs to engage the same principles and encourage individual inquiry, engagement and performance.

This chapter examines the hopes of standardized curricula and the
fallacies it presents for all students' learning styles and cognitive devel-

opment. It looks at the broken promise of promoting twenty-first-century learners in a classroom where passing a test has overshadowed the real meaning of education.

In 2010 the American Association of Colleges for Teacher Education (AACTE) published a document outlining the twenty-first-century skills necessary for students in P–12.

Requirements for twenty-first-century skills still embrace core academic understanding and knowledge. Without basic skills, critical thinking and problem solving cannot take place. The abilities to think critically, explore, debate, communicate, collaborate, and discover new information are the essence of an expanding mind ready for an expanding universe.

When a classroom, school, or district calls for the implementation of this framework, teachers respond with enthusiasm. They build on existing skills and promote newfound knowledge combined with ongoing assessments of all types, support systems, and professional growth and development. In return, the students become more engaged, invested, and excited about learning.

Let's face it: we no longer live in a manufacturing mode with assembly lines made up of trained, but unskilled, workers repeating one small task to create a whole. Robots have eliminated the need for much of the unskilled assembly-line labor force of the past. And yet we are prepping our students to take assembly line–like tests to determine their readiness for the next grade. We are ignoring our students with potential to adhere to regulations for inclusionary classes and missing the opportunity to use the talents of our teachers to the best advantage for the education of our youth.

AMERICAN ASSOCIATION OF COLLEGES FOR TEACHER EDUCATION (AACTE)

How can our colleges and universities help move education in our country forward? AACTE cites the following as essential for new teacher education:

- Mastery of core subjects and twenty-first century themes are essential to student success. Core subjects that include English, reading or language arts, world languages, arts, mathematics, economics, science, geography, history, government, and civics.

Promoting an understanding of academic content at much higher levels by weaving twenty-first century interdisciplinary themes into core subjects:

- Global Awareness
- Financial, Economic, Business, and Entrepreneurial Literacy

- Civic Literacy Health Literacy
- Environmental Literacy Learning and Innovation Skills (AACTE, 2010)

The ability to learn new skills to innovate and adjust to new technologies is necessary for students living in a fast moving and complex life. More than ever, collaboration is essential to problem solve and create new solutions as the need arises. The AACTE's report, *21st Century Knowledge and Skills in Educator Preparation* (2010) lists the following as requirements for teacher preparation:

1. Creativity and Innovation
2. Critical Thinking and Problem Solving
3. Communication and Collaboration
4. Information, Media, and Technology Skills

Our information-, technology-, and media-focused environment demands that our students be ready to adjust to the rapid changes occurring on a daily basis. They must be able to navigate, collaborate, communicate, and function in a highly competitive international market.

The AACTE is very specific on the needs for twenty-first-century classroom teaching, and yet we find ourselves very far behind on international standings. We remain focused on twentieth-century curriculum demands and testing that has little to do with innovative thinking but, rather, demands memorization. The current multiple-choice format seems bent on trickery rather than knowledge.

Teachers should be encouraged and prepared for a more blended-learning classroom, technology, and project-based integration. As Barseghian (2012) claims, "The focus should be on allowing kids to be creators of work that's relevant to their own world—that's what will catapult 'blended learning' out of the next edu-fad and qualify it as a true change agent" (np). So where are college teacher education preparation programs now? How are we creating twenty-first century learning environments for our students, and where are we in comparison to countries that score highest on international tests?

CURRENT STATUS OF TEACHER PREPARATION

Unfortunately the answer is not positive for current teacher education programs and, thus, not positive for many of the public schools in our country. College and university programs are stuck in twentieth-century methodologies and curricula. In a report on teacher preparation programs across the country indicates, Adams and Baron (2013) comment that "Teacher preparation is described as an 'industry of mediocrity that accepts applicants who generally are not high achievers and churn out first year teachers grossly lacking in the' classroom management skills and content knowledge needed to serve students."

Having a child assigned to a first-year teacher can cause learning loss for the year and set them behind their peers in classrooms with more experienced and seasoned teachers. Further damage is done to students in the inner city and public schools with high populations of poor and minority students. First-year teachers are often assigned to places where the more experienced have left for greener pastures. Exacerbating the issue is their lack of training in dealing with students with disabilities, leaving nothing for the potentially average and above average student in the classroom.

Other issues include the demands placed on classroom teachers in public schools where funding is limited and resources scarce. Teachers are now required to teach students who are classified with a disability or speak English as a second language, be fluent in the use of technology, and prepare all to pass standardized tests with perhaps only seven months of instruction.

The National Council on Teacher Quality recently reported on teacher preparation programs in Georgia. They concluded tha, "a vast majority of teacher preparation programs do not give aspiring teachers adequate return on their investment of time and tuition dollars" (quoted in Elliott, 2013, np). Nationwide, only four colleges earned top scores for their secondary education preparation programs. In fact, after more than two years of collecting data and reviewing and analyzing content standards, course manuals, syllabi, and teacher training experiences, they found colleges and other teacher preparation programs have become "an industry of mediocrity, churning out first year teachers with classroom management skills and content knowledge inadequate to thrive in classrooms with ever-increasing ethnic and socioeconomic student diversity" (quoted in Elliott, 2013, np). As Darling-Hammond explains,

> More time is needed to fit in courses that meet new expectations for teachers in dealing with special education, English learners, technology, Common Core standards, child development, content pedagogy, positive discipline, child mental health and everything else we are asked to ensure that teachers learn. (Quoted in Adams & Baron, 2013, np)

To be sure, programs that excel within school districts often have the resources to mentor and support teachers during their first years of teaching. Wealthy districts throughout the country attract teachers from top schools and continue to succeed in providing excellence for their students and their communities. In these districts, teachers are well paid, respected, and provided with the newest resources to assist in their objectives for students.

Unfortunately, too many institutions of higher learning have not changed their programs to keep pace with the rapid advances in educational needs for the twenty-first century. The current system of evaluating teachers based on the "one size fits all" standardized testing has discouraged enrollment in many teacher education programs.

As Bill Gates stated in a BBC News conference in 2007, "One of the most important changes of the last thirty years is that digital technology has transformed almost everyone into an information age worker" (np). A poll taken by the Partnership for 21st Century Skills showed 99 percent of registered voters agreed. In addition, they agreed the basic skills necessary to advance to higher-level skills—understanding and implementing critical thinking and problem solving to communicate through innovative technological systems—are critical to the economic health and growth of the United States (Gates, 2007).

HOW WE COMPARE

From all the news reports and negative publicity about teachers and our education system in the United States, we know that attraction to the profession is in a decline. As a matter of fact, many do not even believe it is a profession but, rather, another staff job ruled regulated by state mandates and driven by standardized testing and the desire for a passing grade for the school and district. Recruiting high-level new teachers has become more and more difficult as the media continues to print negative stories about schools, teachers, and district personnel. And education itself has become a political platform for reform agendas based on constituency instead of need.

Teacher quality is key to the success or failure of our public school system, and, according to Innerst (2007), writing in the *Washington Times*, "The problem with unsatisfactory classroom learning is rooted in the selection and education of students who say they want to be teachers" (p. A2). The result of the media and political criticism of teachers and education as well as the entrenched programs in many teacher education colleges have put our nation in an untenable position of mediocrity.

Other criticisms concern the lack of intellectual rigor in college preparatory course and experiences as well as accusations over the intent to increase revenue rather than the quality of programs. Districts are scrambling to find qualified teachers to fill vacancies in their schools. The problem they are having is documented in New York City's search for teachers in every area, including the much-publicized need in science and math.

A case in point, according to Innerst (2007), was a Long Island district review process for hiring. The school district [received] 758 applications in response to an advertisement—officials decided to narrow the pool by asking applicants to take a short version of a multiple-choice reading comprehension test from the state's 11th grade English Regents exam. Only 202 applicants answered at least 40 of the 50 questions correctly. (p. A2)

In response to all the negative publicity and reactions from the public, many higher institutions of learning have raised the standards for admission and have required a master level in education before entering the classroom. But more needs to be done. What can we learn from the highest-ranking international schools?

Sam Dillon (2011) reported in the *New York Times* on national and public attitudes of teachers in the United States compared to Finland, Korea, and Singapore. These countries only recruit candidates for teaching who have been performing highly in college and provide the supports necessary for successful entry into the classroom. Mentoring, in addition to the student teaching experience, continues until they are confident and competent. Respect for the profession is national; teachers are regarded in the highest regard and are regarded for their service, with continued professional development and salaries commensurate with their status.

In contrast, Republicans in Wisconsin emulate much of the attitude nationwide. They are introducing and supporting legislation to deny bargaining rights and limit taxpayer contributions to their pensions. Arthur Levine (2006) expresses concern that

graduates of teacher preparation programs are poorly prepared for teaching. Concerns include low admissions standards, fewer high-powered professors, and a disorganized teacher education curriculum. The study asserts that as education schools sought to gain respect in the world of higher education, they focused on academic research instead of classroom practice and became isolated from K–12 schools where students are taught. As a result, prospective teachers are not given the tools needed to succeed in an environment where student achievement is the fundamental goal. (p. 36)

No wonder that attracting young, bright people to a teaching career is proving more and more difficult. How can we educate the public and politicians to understand that respecting and supporting teachers is one of the insurance policies for keeping the United States healthy? Public schools are the backbone for future societal success. Funding education, raising standards for teacher recruitment, and supporting educators with respect and fair compensation should be the mantra of the country.

Studying successful programs, expectations, and results in Canada, Finland, Singapore, and South Korea help determine the changes needed to move our teacher preparation programs forward:

1. Alter attitudes about the value of educators is an absolute so we can attract the best and the brightest to the profession.
2. Raise the standard for entrance into teacher education programs nationwide.
3. Increase internships throughout coursework in public schools in all demographic areas.
4. Develop expectations for education faculty research on the most advanced techniques and needs for twenty-first-century skills.
5. Create partnerships between college programs and public schools.
6. Study evaluation processes for other professions and abandon test scores as the means for assessing effectiveness.
7. Provide mentoring for first- and second-year teacher.
8. Provide government funding for all children to attend preschool.
9. Train special education teachers to work with student who have special needs.
10. Increase and standardize salaries and benefits for all teachers, regardless of where they are employed.

CHANGING THE LANDSCAPE

What are the expectations for teachers? According to the Center for High Impact Philanthropy (2010):

> A quality teacher is one who has a positive effect on student learning and development through a combination of content mastery, command of a broad set of pedagogic skills, and communications/interpersonal skills. Quality teachers are lifelong learners in their subject areas, teach with commitment, and are reflective upon their teaching practice. They transfer knowledge of their subject matter and the learning process through good communication, diagnostic skills, understanding of different learning styles and cultural influences, knowledge about child development, and the ability to marshal a broad array of techniques to meet student needs. They set high expectations and support students in achieving them. They establish an environment conducive to learning, and leverage available resources outside as well as inside the classroom. (p. 7)

Simply providing educational pedagogy to a curriculum is not enough to foster competence in the public school system. Raising standards for admission, providing the curricula necessary to address twenty-first-century skills through problem solving, and improving methods of assessment and evaluation are only a beginning.

Changing Demographics

The United States is unique in that is has the most diverse population in the world. Diversity is part of our strength as a nation but demands a different look at the profession of education.

Universities must bring perspectives from different cultures and bring diversity into faculty positions to increase the intellectual outlook of the prospective classroom teacher. Inclusion in the sense of a demographic shift over the last several decades means changing the methodology to increase understanding of the attending cultures in our schools.

Ambrose et al. (2004) points out, "The past 30 years is largely responsible for increased diversity as the population of races other than White or Black grew by the year 2000. . . . The aggregated Minority population increased by 88 %" (p. 2).

The evidence of change demands a different approach to educational courses in our universities. Very few schools in the United States today boast a homogeneous population unless they are private and sectarian in nature. Indicators in table 5.1 show the trends of increased diversity in public schooling.

Today, teachers across the United States must be prepared to meet and teach children from immigrant households. According to Beavers and D'Amico (2005):

> The 2000 census shows that in just ten years the number of children in immigrant families increased by 63 percent. . . . The Latino population (both immigrant and non-immigrant) grew by more than 50 percent and is now the largest group contributing to the nation's diversity. (p. 2)

In response to the increased diversity in our population and schools, teachers are not adequately prepared, nor are colleges and universities up to date on the needs necessary to meet the diversity challenge.

Locale	Total	White	Black	Hispanic	Asian/ Pacific Islander	American Indian/ Alaska Native
Total Number	48,397,895	26,991,389	8,238,245	10,237,009	2,345,968	585,264
City	14,232,071	4,659,317	3,681,265	4,589,508	982,962	119,019
Suburban	16,913,887	9,751,799	2,513,524	3,536,220	1,017,506	94,838
Town	6,097,471	4,218,463	691,804	940,324	115,775	131,105
Rural	11,154,466	8,361,810	1,151,652	1,170,957	2229,725	240,322
Total %	100	55.8	17.0	21.2	4.8	1.2
City	100	32.7	27.3	32.2	6.9	0.8
Suburban	100	57.7	14.9	20.9	6.0	0.6
Town	100	69.2	11.3	15.4	1.9	2.2
Rural	100	75.0	10.3	10.5	2.1	2.2

Courses on cultural differences and language difficulties should serve as introductions to diversity but should not be expected to meet the standards or experience necessary for effective instruction. Increased faculty understanding and knowledge of cultures and linguistics are essential to begin preparation for prospective educators. Colleges themselves need to attract professors from diverse heritages and backgrounds to strengthen education among all minority groups. Collaboration among faculty brings a broad perspective from the experiences and backgrounds of communities of all different cultures.

Allan and Estler (2005) state,

> In the increasingly diverse context of education in the US, most university and college faculty preparing leaders for K–12 or postsecondary settings in the 21st century agree that sensitivity to identity differences and multicultural competence should be essential outcomes of their graduate programs. (p. 209–210)

Table 5.2 presents an expansive background of the diversity born within and outside the United States.

Immigrant and multicultural influence continue to grow each year in our communities and schools. These populations constitute the greatest number of enrollees in our public school system and, according to the U.S. Census, number over five million K–12 students (U.S. Census Bureau, 2013). Reformation of our education system to meet this trend is essential for our economic health and continued leadership in the free world. And while we meet this challenge, we must also reform an outdated education system to meet the needs of all students.

It is nearly impossible to deliver instruction in all of the languages represented at our public schools. The purpose of the ESL (English as a second language) teachers is to support students in their adjustment to a new environment and the learning of mandated content at grade level. In addition to teaching special classes in English, ESL teachers are pushed into general classrooms to help students understand the content being delivered.

Schools of education in colleges and universities should be in the forefront of research seeking the best ways to assure potential achievement for all students. In addition to adding more diversity to faculty, reforming the structure of the college to meet demands of twenty-first century skills is essential. Integrating pedagogy with content from other schools within a university results in dual expertise: content knowledge and eloquence of delivery to the classroom.

Managing the influx of languages other than English is problematic in the current structure of testing and evaluating. Teachers in elementary schools are required to prepare ESL students for tests taken in English, often before the students have reached proficiency in the English language. More attention is required at the university level to help foreign

Race/Ethnicity and Subgroup	Total	Born within the United States	Born Outside the United States		Percentage Distribution
			Number	Percentage	
Total	73,912,900	95.2	3,576,500	4.8	100.0
White	41,955,200	98.2	737,100	1.8	20.6
Black	10,565,400	97.3	290,000	2.7	8.1
Hispanic	15,332,000	88.6	1,751,100	11.4	49.0
Mexican	10,616,900	89.3	1,134,400	10.7	31.7
Puerto Rican	1,334,300	89.5	139,700	10.5	3.9
Cuban	328,400	86.0	46,000	14.0	1.3
Dominican	370,200	82.0	66,700	18.0	1.9
Salvadoran	429,600	86.8	56,800	13.2	1.6
Other Central American	558,700	81.3	104,700	18.8	2.9
South American	609,700	74.3	156,800	25.7	4.4
Other Hispanic or Latino	1,084,300	95.8	46,000	4.2	1.3
Asian	2,886,500	76.1	689,700	23.9	19.3
Asian Indian	623,100	73.3	142,600	22.9	4.0
Chinese	607,600	73.3	162,200	26.7	4.5
Filipino	480,900	76.0	110,800	24.0	3.1
Japanese	84,300	68.2	26,800	31.8	0.8
Korean	287,300	61.2	111,600	38.9	3.1
Vietnamese	372, 100	83.7	60,600	16.3	1.7
Other Asian Native	451,200	83.4	75,000	16.6	2.1
Hawaiian/Pacific	103,900	78.8	22,000	21.2	0.6
Indian/ Alaskan Native	558,700	99.6	2,200	0.4	0.1
Two or more races	2,265,300	97.5	57,600	2.5	2.6

students assimilate, to learn English while attaining content in all subject areas. Perhaps more focus is needed in teaching literacy/language skills in all content areas and providing texts in languages other than English while assimilating into the public school culture.

Special Education

Colleges of education offer dual certification in both regular and special education for the purpose of preparing teachers to instruct all levels of students: those with special needs along with the regular education student. This methodology saves school districts money by asking the classroom teacher to address the needs of all students within her classroom. The impossibility of the task becomes evident as the United States slides down the rankings in international comparison. The U.S. Department of Education (1994) archives reported more than 40 percent of students with special needs were being educated in the general education classroom by 1994.

The No Child Left Behind Act of 2001 demanded 90 percent of students with special needs be tested on the same assessments as their regular education peers. Schools and districts were then evaluated on the scores, causing panic and focus on the wrong goals for education. Colleges and universities jumped to the fore and provided dual certification for teachers previously certified only as regular education teachers. The courses fall short of the intricate knowledge and pedagogy necessary for many of the special needs students.

Should teachers have the knowledge of both traditional and special education needs for its students? Should all learning styles and differentiated instruction be part of the teacher preparation landscape? The answer is, of course, yes! But if we look at the most successful schools, real expertise is focused and implemented to meet the needs of all students in the system. Special education courses should be integrated into general education curricula but should not be relied on for servicing the more intense needs of the student with disabilities. We spend more money incrementally on the results of ineffective education for both special needs and general education students in the long run. Dropouts; disengagement; and lack of readiness for secondary, vocational, or postsecondary education cost society more than dealing with appropriate placement and content mastery in the school setting.

We can no longer try to give our prospective teachers a general knowledge to meet the real needs for real students. Teachers for students with special needs must have the knowledge and training to help students achieve the greatest potential possible. General education teachers must do the same for their general education students.

Inclusion, mandated through IDEA, can work well if properly implemented. A classroom with combinations of students with or without special needs must have two teachers: one for special education and the other for general education. Working together but not weakening the content serves both populations to meet greater success.

Content Expertise

For example, to teach science in a secondary school, many colleges and universities require everyone take at least sixty credits of foundation courses having little or nothing to do with science. It is only after completion of those courses that students get to address concentration in the area to be taught.

Of course, other courses are necessary in pedagogical skills and learning/teaching styles needed for the classroom, but integration of those within the specific content area would be more efficient and meaningful.

And, if inclusion remains the legal mandate for students with special needs, special educators with specific knowledge in that area should be partnered with the content teacher to allow all students reach their potential. What seems to be imperative for all colleges and universities is to examine the findings of the National Council on Teacher Quality (NCTQ) and reform postsecondary education programs so that they compete with the best and produce high-quality educators.

NATIONAL FINDINGS

In 2013, the NCTQ studied 2,420 college teacher preparation programs in the United States to examine practices and criteria for teacher candidate selection as compared to high-performing countries on international assessments. The following lists the findings (NCTQ, 2013b):

- Teacher preparation programs in top-performing countries recruit teacher candidates from the top third of college enrollees. One in four U.S. programs recruit for the top half.
- According to the research, the majority of programs in the United States, (71 percent) do not use practical, research-based methodology in the teaching of literacy, which may be a factor in the 30 percent rate of reading failure at the elementary level.
- Mathematics and science in elementary programs in Singapore and South Korea far surpass the paltry 19 percent rate of excellence in the United States. Expectations for teachers in high-ranking countries include mastery of knowledge in both math and science.
- Almost all programs (93 percent) "fail to ensure a high-quality student teaching experience, where candidates are assigned only to highly skilled teachers and must receive frequent concrete feedback" (p. 2).
- Management strategies for classrooms that improve the behavioral environment are lacking. Of the rated programs, only 23 percent addressed classroom management to their teacher candidates in detail.
- Secondary-level content preparation is inadequate; only 47 percent, less than half, are providing the necessary knowledge for teachers in the subjects they are or will be teaching.

Figures 5.1 and 5.2 indicate, by percentage ratings, preparation for teachers in select categories for both elementary and secondary schools in the United States.

Indications from the graphs in figures 5.1 and 5.2 leave little doubt that we must address our teacher preparation programs if we are to remain competitive in the world marketplace intellectually and socioeconomically.

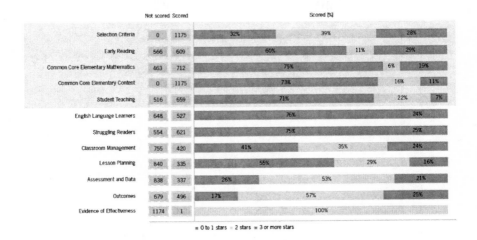

	Not scored	Scored	Scored [%]		
Selection Criteria	0	1175	32%	39%	28%
Early Reading	566	609	60%	11%	29%
Common Core Elementary Mathematics	463	712	75%	6%	19%
Common Core Elementary Content	0	1175	73%	16%	11%
Student Teaching	516	659	71%	22%	7%
English Language Learners	648	527	76%		24%
Struggling Readers	554	621	75%		25%
Classroom Management	755	420	41%	35%	24%
Lesson Planning	840	335	55%	29%	16%
Assessment and Data	838	337	26%	53%	21%
Outcomes	679	496	17%	57%	25%
Evidence of Effectiveness	1174	1	100%		

■ 0 to 1 stars ■ 2 stars ■ 3 or more stars

Figure 5.1.   National Elementary Teacher Prep Rating Distribution

CHANGING OUR PARADIGM FOR TEACHER PREPARATION

We must implore government—local, state, and national—to remove the stringent assessments that have become the guide for the implementation of programs in public schools. Studying the most successful evaluation practices internationally can serve as models for informed assessments to develop curricula and implementation that serve the needs of all students within the public school system.

Stigmatizing teachers, schools, and districts based on a one-size-fits-all standardized instrument continues to frustrate those teachers who remain in education and discourage those who may have an interest in teaching as a profession.

Revolutionizing our teacher education programs in colleges and universities is a must if the United States is to survive as a world leader that influences trends for peace, socioeconomic reform, and technological advances. When are we going to wake up?

THE POWER OF PARTNERSHIPS

Partnerships with major colleges within the university framework can offer prospective teachers more focus on areas of interest and strength. Education courses focusing on pedagogy should be integrated within the framework of content areas suited for middle and secondary schools. Perhaps we should be looking at the integration of all colleges within the university to enhance not only knowledge of content but practices to

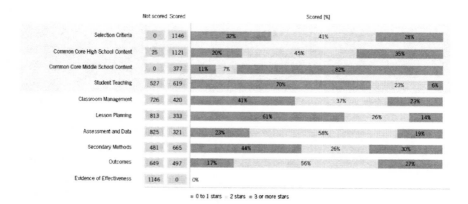

Figure 5.2.   National Secondary Teacher Prep Rating Distribution. *Source: National Council on Teacher Quality (NCTQ) Teacher Prep, http://www.nctq.org/teacherprep/findings/.*

improve the teaching skills of all professors, regardless of specific areas of expertise.

For example, some evidence from research suggests postsecondary education programs "can equip their graduates to boost student achievement in mathematics by ensuring they have completed subject-specific coursework including pedagogical content" (Harris & Sass, 2007; Rice, 2003). In addition, schools of education need to focus on literacy in all subject areas. Literacy is an understanding of language, math, science, social studies, and literature, regardless of the content area.

Early childhood education is an area of importance for colleges and universities to attend to. Early education impacts all future opportunities for learning and intellectual growth. ESL learners and children living in poor environments can increase their cognitive potential through professional early childhood programs. According to the Rauch Foundation (2013), 85 percent of the brain is developed by five years of age. And Pianta and Hadden (2008) stress the importance of focusing "beyond a reliance on early-childhood credentials. . . . The substance and content of the training program play the largest role in improving results for children" (p. 25). Colleges and universities need research to develop more comprehensive programs in training early childhood educators.

The lower incidence of special education classification, dropout rates, and disengagement at the secondary level can be traced back to early education experiences. In top-ranking countries, funding for preschool is at government expense, teachers are trained professionals in early education, and every child is given the opportunity and expectation to attend. Early education should be taught as developmental and cognitive sciences in colleges and universities to apply the best-researched principles in directed teaching/learning for the young mind.

So many studies have been done on the importance of early childhood education, but how many colleges and universities actually study neuroscience when preparing early childhood educators? According to the National Scientific Council on the Developing Child (2012), "The basic principles of neuroscience indicate that early preventative intervention will be more efficient and produce more favorable outcomes than remediation later in life" (p. 8).

In addition, understanding the development of the adolescent for middle and high school teachers is essential while developing curricula and implementation strategies for successful achievement. The fragmentation of focus at the college teacher preparation level leaves large gaps in understanding the progression of development from early childhood through later adolescence.

Connection to the sciences and psychology departments in colleges and universities would provide a whole picture of teaching/learning. What would it look like if all prospective teachers had to spend time in early childhood, elementary, middle, and high school settings? Partnering with schools housing all levels provides the experience of seeing the whole child and how development makes a difference in a child's success in school.

Adding pre-internships in public schools prior to student teaching should be requirements and part of the overall curriculum. Teacher candidates need to be familiar with the setting in terms of culture, language, socioeconomic environment, and specific needs within the community. One of the biggest issues in urban education housing more poor and immigrant families is the lack of understanding among schools and teachers on the needs and how to address them. Mulvey and Cooper (2012) conclude, "The characteristics of a neighborhood influence the climate inside and outside of the family. . . . Unsafe and unsavory environments are manifested in depression and lower cognitive functioning" (p. 124).

Partnerships among health educators, social workers, community leaders, and schools of education can bring real reform and change to the so-labeled "failing schools." Instead of privatizing preschools, as recently suggested by districts on Long Island, prepare quality early childhood programs to ready children for successful school lives. Promote research into the development phases of cognition and mental prowess and bring that knowledge to communities that need it most.

CONCLUSION

What would teacher education look like?

The United States is in the throes of a downward spiral educationally. Our schools are not fulfilling the needs of future leaders, businessmen, entrepreneurs, inventors, health-care professionals, politicians, and/or teachers. We are in the need of a revolution in our public schools, colleges, and universities. As Sir Ken Robinson points out in his 2010 TED Talk:

> The argument lies in the poor education and preparation of the teacher, not the broken state of our public schools. Many teachers are inadequate for the student's needs in the classroom because they do not try to work with what they have to make things interesting. Universities and colleges need to work to prepare teachers by giving them more in-field training and learning situations as well as offering more rigorous training in subjects that are taught in schools (learn from Finland). Teachers who are not masters in their subject have no passion for it, and passion is one of the most important subjects teachers can pass to their students.

What would our teacher preparation look like if we followed a system that respected and attracted some of the top students in academia for our public schools? As public schools move toward integration of disabled students into general education classroom, the professional responsibilities of general education teachers and principals are being redefined" (Fritz & Miller, 1995, p. 299).

REFERENCES

Adams, J. M., & Baron, K. (2013). Critical report on teacher preparation programs sparks debate. *Ed Source*. Retrieved from http://edsource.org/today/ 2013/critical-report-on-teacher-preparation-programs-sparks-debate/33721#.Un5VRiihDHg.

Allan, E. J., & Estler, S. E. (2005). Diversity, privilege, and us: Collaborative transformation among educational leadership faculty. *Innovative Higher Education, 29*(3) 209–232.

Ambrose, S., Bridges, M., Clark, M., Dawes, R., Nair, I., Pataki, S., Resnick, D., Tademy, E., & Trotter, J. (2004). *The benefits of diversity education at Carnegie Mellon.* Pittsburgh, PA: President's Diversity Advisory Council, Carnegie Mellon.

American Association of Colleges for Teacher Education (AACTE). (2010). *21st century knowledge and skills in educator preparation.* Washington, DC: American Association of Colleges for Teacher Education.

Barseghian, T. (2012, November 13). Blended learning: Passing fad or true innovation. *Mind/Shift*. Retrieved from http://blogs.kqed.org/mindshift/2012/11/blended-learning-passing-fad-or-true-innovation/.

Beavers, L., & D'Amico, J. D. (2005). *Children in immigrant families: U.S. and state-level findings from the 2000 Census.* Baltimore: The Annie E. Casey Foundation.

Center for High Impact Philanthropy. (2010). *High impact philanthropy to improve teacher quality in the US.* Philadelphia, PA: University of Pennsylvania.

Dillon, S. (2011, March 16). U.S. is urged to raise teachers' status. *New York Times*, p. A22.

Duncan, A. (2009, October 22). *Colleges of Education must improve for reforms to succeed.* Press Release, U.S. Department of Education.

Elliott, P. (2013, June 18). Too many teachers, too little quality. *Salt Lake Tribune*. Retrieved from http://www.sltrib.com/sltrib/mobile/56476557-68/programsteachersteacher-students.html.csp.

Fritz, M., & Miller, M. (1995). Challenges of the inclusive classroom. *Contemporary Education* 66(4), 294–309.

Gates, B. (2007, December 14). Bill Gates: The skills you need to succeed. *BBC News* online. Retrieved from http://news.bbc.co.uk/2/hi/7142073.stm.

Hanushek, E. A., Peterson, P. E., & Woessman, L. (2012). *Achievement growth: International and U.S. trends in student performance.* Cambridge, MA: Program on Education Policy and Governance and Education Next, Harvard University.

Harris, D. N., & Sass, T. R. (2007). "Teacher training, teacher quality, and student achievement." CALDER Working Paper 3. Washington, DC: The Urban Institute.

Innerst, C. (2007). Schools of education seen failing. *Washington (DC) Times*, p. A2.

Levine, A. (2006). *Educating school teachers.* Washington, DC: Education School Project.

Mulvey, J., & Cooper, B. (2012). *Intersections of children's health education and welfare.* New York: Palgrave Macmillan.

National Center for Education Statistics. (2008). Common core of date (CCD): Public elementary/secondary school universe survey, 2007–2008. Washington, DC: U.S. Department of Education.

National Council on Teacher Quality (NCTQ). (2013a). *Teacher prep review: A review of the nation's teacher preparation programs.* Washington, DC: National Council on Teacher Quality.

National Council on Teacher Quality (NCTQ). (2013b). Findings from the Teacher Prep Review. Retrieved from http://www.nctq.org/teacherPrep/findings.

National Scientific Council on the Developing Child. (2012). *The science of early childhood development.* Cambridge, MA: Center on the Developing Child, Harvard University.

Pianta, R. C., & Hadden, D. S. (2008). What we know about the quality of early childhood settings: Implications for research on teacher preparation and professional development. *The State Education Standard*, 20–27.

Rauch Foundation. (2013). Starting at the beginning. http://www.rauchfoundation.org/how-we-work-/what-we-support.

Rice, J. (2003). Teacher quality: Understanding the effectiveness of teacher attributes. Economic Policy Institute.

Robinson, K. (2010). Bring on the learning revolution [video file]. Retrieved from http://www.ted.com/talks/sir_ken_robinson_bring_on_the_revolution.

United States Census Bureau. (2007). *American community survey.* Washington, DC: U.S. Department of Commerce.

United States Census Bureau. (2013). *Multicultural education history.* Washington, DC: U.S. Department of Commerce. http://education.stateuniversity.com/pages/2252/multi-cultural-education.html.

U.S. Dept. of Education. (1994). In: Hocutt, A. (2004) *Effectiveness of special education: Is placement the critical factor.* http://www.princeton.edu/futureofchildren/publication/docs06_01_04.pdf.

SIX

Level of Instruction in Each Setting

Karen Gagliardi

The reauthorization of the No Child Left Behind Act (2008) has reemphasized the policy to integrate students with special needs into the general education classroom. According to the United States Department of Education (2006), approximately 80 percent of students with disabilities receive educational support in the general education classroom.

When disabled students are integrated into general education classrooms, a major concern that emerges is the potential impact of attitudes of regular classroom teachers toward these students (Garvar-Pinhas & Schmelkin, 1989). The attitudes and behaviors of educators toward any individual student can either enable the pupil to progress intellectually, socially, or emotionally, or can inhibit the child's opportunities for learning and growth. A significant portion of the literature on inclusion indicates that general education teachers generally feel ill prepared to handle the various special needs of the student in their classrooms (Lewis, 1994). Many teachers believe that they have not been given adequate time to learn how to work with students with disabilities before implementation occurred (D'Alonzo & Giordano, 1996). Myles and Simpson (1989) reported that 85 percent of the general educators they surveyed were willing to accept a student with disabilities in their classrooms on a full-time basis, given appropriate training. Without support and training, less that 33 percent of the respondents were willing to accept these students in their general education classes.

"Jean" teaches fifth grade in a general education classroom. She has taught at the elementary level in the district for twenty-five years. She has been at Robert E. Lee Elementary for the past eleven years.

Jean has a special education instructional assistant who works with her for 2 hours a day. She appeared to be generally positive about working with students with disabilities; however, she spoke about her obligation to teach all of the children in her class. She shared her own experiences of working with student with emotional disabilities who she felt were not adequately prepared to be integrated into a general education classroom. She indicated that she feels integration for most students with disabilities can be successful if proper accommodations are made and if the administrators provide the necessary support. I think special education students should only be in the regular classroom if they have basic academic understanding for what is going on. If their behavior severely interrupts the learning process, I don't think they should be mainstreamed. (Morgan, 2011)

WHAT DOES LEAST RESTRICTIVE ENVIRONMENT MEAN?

According to the 2009 United States Census Bureau, over 7 percent of American children ages three to seventeen suffer from a learning disability. Due to the Individuals with Disabilities Education Act (IDEA), these children are entitled to an education in the least restrictive environment (LRE). Before this legislation was passed, children were often segregated from the public school. The first major stepping-stone into special education, however, was the case of *Brown v. Board of Education* in 1954 (hereafter *Brown*). Least restrictive environment (LRE) is the federal law that mandates students with disabilities receive their education, to the maximum extent appropriate, with nondisabled peers and that special education students are not removed from regular classes unless, even with supplemental aids and services, education in regular classes cannot be achieved satisfactorily. IDEA was passed and entitled children to a "free appropriate public education, which emphasizes special education and related services designed to meet their unique needs" (Mostert & Crockett, 2010, p. 1). With this, over sixty-one million students across America are attending school with some type of disability (U.S. Census Bureau, 2009). Both *Brown* and IDEA "asserted the need for increased educational opportunities" for students with a disability and claimed, "segregation was inherently harmful and unequal" (Ferri & Connor, 2005, p. 1). This helped lead students into the public school setting in their least restrictive environment.

MAINSTREAMING, INTEGRATION, FULL INCLUSION, AND REVERSE MAINSTREAMING

None of these terms appears or is defined in federal or state statutes. They are terms that have been developed by educators to describe various ways of meeting the LRE requirement of special education. As a result, different educational agencies—school districts, county offices or special education local planning areas—may have somewhat different definitions of these terms.

By definition, *mainstreaming* refers to placement of a student with disabilities into ongoing activities or regular classrooms so that the child receives education with nondisabled peers—even if special education staff must provide supplementary resource services. Integration includes mainstreaming into regular classes and access to, inclusion in, and participation in the activities of the total school environment.

Integration combines placement in public schools with ongoing structured and unstructured opportunities to interact with nondisabled peers. A student with severe disabilities should be able to participate in many general school activities, such as lunch, assemblies, clubs, dances, or recess. The student should be able to participate in selected activities in regular classes, such as art, music, or computers. The student should be able to participate in regular academic subjects in regular classes if appropriate curriculum modifications are made and adequate support is provided. The student should be able to use the same facilities as nondisabled students, including hallways, restrooms, libraries, cafeterias, and gymnasiums. Integration can refer to integration of a special education student in the regular education classroom in the same sense as in mainstreaming. However, integration also refers to placement of students in special education classes located on integrated school sites (that is, sites that have both special and regular education classes). Integrated placement includes systematic efforts to maximize interaction between the student with disabilities and nondisabled peers.

Full inclusion refers to the total integration of a student with disabilities into the regular education program, with special support. In full inclusion, the student's primary placement is in the regular education class. The student has no additional assignment to any special class for student with disabilities. Thus, the student with disabilities is actually a member of the regular education class. She is not being integrated or mainstreamed into the regular education class from a special day class. The student need not be in class 100 percent of the time and can leave the class to receive supplementary services, such as speech or physical therapy.

Reverse mainstreaming refers to the practice of giving opportunities to interact with nondisabled peers to students who are placed in a self-contained or segregated classroom (or school) or who lives and attends school at a state hospital. It brings nondisabled students to a segregated site or to state hospital classrooms for periods of time to work with or tutor students with disabilities. School districts attempt to fulfill the LRE mandates by using reverse mainstreaming exclusively. They should make systemic efforts to get students with disabilities out of special classrooms and into the school's integrated environments. Reverse mainstreaming alone is an artificial means of integration. The Individual Education Program (IEP) team might consider placements that encourage natural interaction with nondisabled peers.

INCLUSION: NEITHER FREE NOR APPROPRIATE

Requiring all disabled children to be included in mainstream classrooms, regardless of their ability to function there, is not only unrealistic but also downright harmful—often to the children themselves, according to Shanker (1995).

What happens when a fourth-grade teacher with a class of thirty or thirty-five finds that several new students have behavioral disabilities? The teacher has no previous training in working with disabled children, and the principal says that getting extra classroom help is out of the question—the school district simply can't afford it. The teacher's main resource, the special education aide, who must serve sixty students in four schools, is stretched pretty thin. As the year goes on, the teacher finds that math class is disrupted every single day by the demand of the special needs students. Many teachers are facing problems as difficult as this as they deal with full inclusion models by law, according to Shanker (1995).

Inclusion—the idea that all children, including those with disabilities, should and can learn in a regular classroom—has taken root in many school systems, although it is not specifically required by law. To oppose inclusion would seem to advocate exclusion. Yet some observers maintain that full inclusion isn't always the best way to meet students' needs. Critics of full inclusion ask whether even students with the most severe disabilities benefit from placement in regular classrooms. Further, some outgrowths of inclusion involve rethinking the structure of the regular classroom. Inclusive classes may require more than one teacher. Specific technology may be needed to help students with disabilities perform better.

In contrast, the National Association for State Boards of Education (NASBE) strongly endorses the "full inclusion" of student with disabilities in regular classrooms. In 1992, NASBE released a report titled, "Winners All: A Call for Inclusive Schools." The report called on states to revise teacher licensure ad certification rules so that new teachers would be prepared to teach children with disabilities as well as those without disabilities. It also recommended training programs to help special educators and regular educators adapt to collaborating in the classroom. Another organization that has approved a resolution supporting inclusion is the Association for Supervision and Curriculum Development (ASCD).

Some organizations endorse goals that assume inclusion is a given. One such group, the Consortium on Inclusive Schooling Practices, states that it focuses on "systemic reform rather than changes in special education policy only" (CCSSO, 1996).

The consortiums' three broad goals are:

- To establish a change process in multiple states focused on systemic reform;
- To translate research and policy information into implementable educational practices;
- To develop the capacity of state and local agencies to provide full inclusive educational services.

"Examine all sides of the debate, and it becomes clear that inclusion is a microcosm of education reform," maintains an essay, "To the Best of Their Abilities" (Teacher Magazine, 1995). The issues extend far beyond special education. "All children can learn at high levels" has become the rallying cry for improving schools. How can policy makers, practitioners, and parents work together to ensure that students in every classroom in every school are achieving that ideal?

While few educators oppose inclusion completely, some express reservations about how full inclusion works in classrooms. Albert Shanker, writer for the American Federation of Teachers in 1996, in "Where We Stand" asserts, "What full inclusionists don't see is that children with disabilities are individuals with differing needs; some benefit from the inclusion and others do not. Full inclusionists don't see that medically fragile children and children with severe behavioral disorders are more likely to be harmed when they are placed in regular classrooms where teachers do not have the highly specialized training to deal with their needs."

Advocates for full inclusion raise the issue of equality. They say that disabled youngsters have an additional handicap when they are segregated from their nondisabled peers because they deserve a chance to develop the social and academic skills necessary to function in the mainstream. Local school boards, state departments of education, and legislators also back full inclusion for different reasons. They see it as an opportunity to cut back on expensive special education services that have become a crushing burden, especially because Congress has not been funding at the level promised by IDEA, leaving states and local school boards to absorb the costs.

The Fourteenth Amendment of the U.S. Constitution has helped laws politicians pass laws like IDEA. As the amendment states, "No State shall make or enforce any law which shall abridge the privileges or immunities of citizens of the United States" (U.S. Const., Amen. XIV, 1). Therefore, states never had the right to hold children with special needs away for the educational system. These children are citizens who are entitled to "life, liberty, and property" with due process of law (U.S. Const. Amend XIV, 1). With this amendment, the Constitution has served as a tool to get further legislation passed that enables children to start in their LRE. Though it serves a great purpose for special education today, two hundred years ago it was not looked on in regard to children with special needs. According to Van Drenth (2005), if children had disabilities they were pushed aside and given "terms such as imbeciles" and "idiots" (p. 1). It has taken America a long time to get away from such treatment. The past fifty years have evolved the way children with special needs are looked on and treated in society. Today IDEA mandates that students be provided with free and appropriate education (FAPE). This appropriate education includes other general education settings.

The appropriate education is determined for each child in his or her individualized education program (IEP). The IEP serves as "the legal roadmap for the development and implementation of every major component of the educational progress for a child with a disability" (Hulett, 2009, p. 145). Therefore, it is intended to lay out the all the necessary "needs, requirements, services, and accommodations" that will best serve the child's educational needs. (Hulett, 2009, p. 145). The IEP is used to ensure that the student is placed in his LRE. According to IDEA, the LRE "is the legal linchpin that ensures that educators and families continually strive to include all students with disabilities no matter the severity of their disabilities in the regular education setting and with their agepeers to the maximum extent appropriate" (Hulett, 2009, p. 147). Just as each child is different, so is his LRE. For some children, the least restrictive environment may be a general education classroom with extra help in a certain subject through a special education classroom. For other students, LRE may be spending half a day, or even a full day, in the special education classroom. Whichever location is chosen for the student through the IPE, it is one that allows that child to spend as much time as possible with his or her typically developing peers.

In addition to LRE, IDEA states that all children are entitled to a FAPE, which is broken down in four implications: social education must (1) be provided at public expense; (2) meet the standards of the state educational agency; (3) include the involvement of an appropriate preschool, elementary school, or secondary school; and (4) conform to IDEA (Hulett, 2009, p. 31– 32). Each child's IEP must depict what is considered an appropriate education for that student. The term *appropriate* is not defined by Congress and can often be difficult to determine from child to child. It does not necessarily mean the best possible education but, rather, the best within reason for aiding the child for success in life.

THE RIGHTS OF STUDENTS WITH DISABILITIES

Though the Constitution provides the foundation of laws and rulings in the United States, it mentions nothing on the subject of education. The

Tenth Amendment, however, states that any powers not given to the national government or not prohibited by the states are given to the states (U.S. Const., Amend X, 1). With this, the rulings for education are given entirely to the individual states. To fund the schools, states refer to the general welfare clause written in article 1 of the Constitution, giving Congress the ability to tax in order to provide for the general welfare of the nation (U.S. Const., article 1.8).

The Fourteenth Amendment also impacts education in that children are not to be denied their right to "life, liberty, and property" (U.S. Const., Amend. XIV, 1). Education is something that is given to each person; therefore, it falls into the category of a person's property. As property, education is a guaranteed right for all people under the Fourteenth Amendment of the U.S. Constitution. The Fourteenth Amendment has been tested in court. During *Brown*, the Supreme Court declared the separation of whites and blacks to be unconstitutional, citing violation of the Fourteenth Amendment (Hulett, 2009, p. 20).

The Supreme Court determined segregation in school denied children equal access to education. When the civil rights movement began sweeping the nation, people started thinking of segregation in all areas of life, not just racial discrimination. People began to question the treatment of children with disabilities and the segregation they received at the time. In the early 1960s, segregation cases were taken to courts throughout the country. Like the ruling in *Brown*, the court began favoring students based on the Fourteenth Amendments rights to property and therefore, an education (Hulett, 2009, p. 20–21). Finally in 1975, President Ford signed Public Law No. 94-142, the Education of All Handicapped Children Act, later renamed IDEA. This act granted each child a FAPE in the LRE, which was drawn out and explained through IEP.

IDEA contained major mandates that have resulted in challenges in court such as *Daniel R.R. v. State Board of Education* (1989, hereafter *Daniel R.R.*). Daniel R.R. was a six-year-old student with Down syndrome. According to his IEP, Daniel was to be placed half a day in a general education preschool and half a day in a special education class. He struggled in the general education classroom and worked better in the special education room. When his IEP team attempted to place him in the special education classroom for the full day, except for recess and lunch, his parents were upset and took the school to court. The Fifth Circuit Court ruled that the "most appropriate setting superseded placement in the regular setting" (1989, *Daniel R.R.*). Therefore, the court ruled in favor of the school and kept Daniel in the special education classroom. This ruling accepted that Daniel was being placed in his own LRE. The court felt that if the special education classroom benefitted the student's education more than the general education classroom, then that child needed to be placed in the special education classroom.

In 1994, another case, *Sacramento City Unified School District v. Rachel H* (1994 hereafter, *Rachel H.*) was filed. Rachel Holland was an eleven-year-old student with a moderate mental disability. She was placed in special education classroom though the beginning of her schooling. Her parents requested that she be integrated with her typically developing peers, and the school offered to include Rachel in nonacademic classes with her peers. Rachel's parents disagreed with the option and requited a hearing. When the hearing officer agreed with Rachel's family, the school went to court. The district court sided with Rachel's parents and developed a test to determine the LRE, now known as the Rachel H Four Factor Test. (1994, *Rachel H.*). This test helped the court reach its verdict, which allowed Rachel to take part in general education academic classes with supplemental services and aids. Because Rachel's parents tried to get their daughter's classroom adjusted, Rachel was no longer held back and was able to learn alongside her typically developing peers. In addition, a new test for the LRE was set in place for the district court to use in future cases.

THE CLASSROOM AND LRE

Michelle Barnes is a third-grade teacher. She has a diverse mix of students in her class, including English language learners; students who are above level, on level, or below level; and students who have disabilities. Ms. Barnes always has taken pride in being a solid teacher. Lately she had felt overwhelmed by competing demands to help all of her students meet the same academic standards and demands to accommodate the need of an increasingly diverse population.

Tyler is a student with learning disabilities in Ms. Barnes's class. His literacy skills are at a beginning third-grade level. Vanessa, another student in the class, functions more like a beginning seventh-grader. In addition to the obvious skill differences between these students, there is great diversity with respect to how these students learn best. Tyler and Vanessa represent just the tip of the iceberg in terms of the wide range of need in Ms. Barnes's class. In the spring, all of Ms. Barnes's students will be expected to take the same state assessment designed to measure student performance against new common core standards for third-graders. Ms. Barnes is left asking herself, "What is the best way to accommodate each students' individual learning needs while simultaneously teaching the same standards for everyone?"

Ms. Barnes is not alone in her lamenting. With the passage of the No Child Left Behind Act, there has been increasing emphasis on the use of large-scale tests to monitor students' progress toward meeting educational standards and hold schools and teachers accountable for this progress. At the same time, other educational trends, such as including more students with disabilities and more English language learners into general education classes, are making our classrooms more diverse than ever before.

For teachers who are left wondering how to satisfy these seemingly contradictory needs of both standards-based reform and inclusion, many questions are often raised: How do I meet the needs of such a wide range of learners? How can I meet each child's individual needs and work toward the same goals?

In response to this challenge, teachers are mandated to implement an ever-increasing array of educational practices. Too often there is no understanding of how these practices are related or even support each other. Teachers also don't know how the overarching goals fit together in the big picture to maximize educational outcomes for all students.

Nearly half of all students in U.S. public schools (42 percent) are students of color, approximately 20 percent of students speak a language other than English at home, and approximately 14 percent of students have an identified disability (U.S. Department of Education 2007a). Approximately half of the students who have an identified disability spend 80 percent of their school day in general education classrooms (U.S. Department of Education 2007b). To add to this diversity, approximately 12 percent of students in public schools are labeled gifted and talented (Friend & Cook, 2007). Like their peers with disabilities, gifted and talented students are also integrated into general education classrooms.

Despite the fact that it is not always possible to get all students to exactly the same point in the curriculum at exactly the same time, it is feasible to move most students through curriculum toward standards. While raising standards is not the same thing as raising expectations, some educators feel that the accountability assessments associated with standards-based reform will force the issue of higher expectations. It is possible that we will have to change our behaviors and adjust our attitudes and expectations. The core idea of not underestimating students' abilities is implicit in standards-based reform and holds particular importance in the education of diverse learners (Voltz, Sims, & Nelson, 2010).

The goals of helping all students meet rigorous standards can only be attained by attending to the needs of the most vulnerable students— students with disabilities and students from culturally diverse background. While standards-based reform is largely silent on the issue of instructional methodology, the inclusion and teaching for cultural and linguistic diversity movements infuse instructional approaches that maximize opportunities for all students to learn from their diverse peers. These approaches include differentiated instruction, universal design, sheltered instruction, and multicultural education.

Differentiated Instruction

Differentiated instruction is an example of a supporting instructional approach that embraces the needs of academically diverse populations — in particular, students who are gifted or who have disabilities. Differentiated instruction involves creating multiple paths to learning for diverse students (Tomlinson, 1999).

Universal Design for Learning

Universal design is an instructional approach that gives particular attention to students who have physical, sensory, and cognitive disabilities. Like differentiated instruction, universal design embraces the idea that instruction should be designed from the beginning with the students' diverse needs in mind. Universal design supports the thought that educators should not have to retrofit lessons for students with exceptional needs after those lessons have already been created. According to Orkwis (1999), "Universal design implies a design of instructional materials and activities that allows learning goals to be attainable by individuals with a wide range of difference in their abilities to see, speak, hear, move, write, understand English, attend, organize, engage, and remember" (p. 1). With universal design, it is important that learning activities provide multiple means of representation or modes of learning. Learning activities also must allow students to respond in various modes and should be designed to engage learners with varying interests and aptitudes. Often educators use assistive technology to implement universal design to make instruction accessible for a broader array of students. Assistive technology refers to "any item, piece of equipment, or product system, whether acquired commercially or off the shelf, modified, or customized that is used to increase, maintain, or improve functional capabilities of a child with a disability" (U.S. Department of Education, 2004, 20 U.S.C. 1401 [a] [25] [IDEA]). Hence, low-tech devices such as pencil grips may be considered assistive technology as well as high-tech devices such as screen readers or electronic books. The principles of universal design are important to engineering classrooms that support diverse learners, including those students with physical, sensory, and cognitive disabilities.

SHELTERED INSTRUCTION

Like differentiated instructional and universal design, sheltered instruction embraces the needs of diverse learners, specifically English language learners. Echevarria, Vogt, and Short (2004) define sheltered instruction by using the following eight broad elements: (1) preparation, (2) building background, (3) comprehensible input, (4) strategies, (5) interaction, (6) practice and application, (7) lesson delivery, and (8) review and assessment. The preparation element suggests that teachers first identify lesson objectives aligned with standards. The building background element requires that teachers link new content to students' background experiences and helps students focus on unfamiliar vocabulary. With the comprehendible input element, as the name implies, teachers use controlled vocabulary, sentence structure, and visuals and gestures to facilitate students' comprehension. The strategy element refers to teaching students different approaches for organizing and retaining information associated with effective learning. The interaction element shows teachers how to structure opportunities for students to interact with the peers during the learning process. The interaction phase leads to the practice and application element, which requires teachers to provide frequent opportunities for students to practice new language skills. The lesson delivery element illustrates how teachers can appropriately pace the lesson and provide for active engagement. The review and assessment element focuses on establishing standards and including language and content-based evaluations. All of these elements are important in designing classroom instruction that embraces the needs of English language learners (Echevarria, Vogt, & Short, 2004).

MULTICULTURAL EDUCATION

Multicultural education is another approach that is important in today's diverse, standards-based classrooms. As the name implies, multicultural education addresses the needs of culturally diverse population of students. Banks (2001) defined this approach with the following five major dimensions: (1) content integration, (2) the knowledge construction profess, (3) bias reduction, (4) empowering school culture, and (5) equity pedagogy. Content integration implies that curricula should include content about diverse populations and present information from diverse points of view. The knowledge construction process focuses on the extent to which teachers explore how knowledge is constructed and how attitudes are formed in regard to what constitutes valuable or important knowledge. Bias reduction refers to activities that are designed to examine and reduce bias attitudes. Building an empowering school culture eradicates systemic factors such as negative effects of tracking practices on diverse groups of students. Equity pedagogy helps teachers use instructional strategies that embrace the learning characteristics and cognitive styles of diverse populations. Multicultural education supports educators in enhancing the educational experiences of all learners, including students from culturally diverse backgrounds.

WHAT MAKES A SCHOOL SUCCESSFUL? RESOURCES, POLICIES, AND PRACTICES

According to the Organisation for Economic Cooperation and Development's Program for International Student Assessment (PISA), school is where most learning happens; what happens in school has a direct impact on learning. In turn, the resources, policies, and practices approved at higher administrative levels in a country's education system influence what happens in school (OECD, 2010).

Successful school systems—those that perform above average and show below-average socioeconomic inequalities—provide all students, regardless of their socioeconomic backgrounds, with similar opportunities to learn. Systems that show high performance and an equitable distribution of learning outcomes tend to be comprehensive, requiring teachers and schools to embrace diverse student populations through personalized educational pathways. In contrast, school systems that assume that students have different destinations with different expectations and differentiation in terms of how they are placed in schools, classes, and grades often show less equitable outcomes without an overall performance advantage. Earlier PISA assessments showed these expectations to be mirrored in how students perceived their own educational future. The results of these differences can also be seen in the distribution of student performance within countries and in the impact that socioeconomic background has on learning outcomes:

- In countries, and in schools within countries, where more students repeat grades, overall results tend to be worse.
- In countries where more students repeat grades, socio-economic differences in performance tend to be wider, suggesting that people from lower socio-economic groups are more likely to be negatively affected by grade repetition.
- In countries where 15-year-olds are divided into more tracks based on their abilities, overall performance is not enhanced, and the younger the age at which selection for such tracks first occurs, the greater the differences in student performance, by socio-economic background, by age 15, without improved overall performance.
- In school systems where it is more common to transfer weak or disruptive students out of a school, performance and equity both tend to be lower. Individual schools that make more use of transfers also perform worse in some countries. (OECD, 2010, p. 12)

These associations account for a substantial amount of the differences in the outcomes of schooling systems. For example, the frequency with which students are transferred across schools is associated with a third of the variation in country performance. This does not necessarily mean that if transfer policies were changed, a third of country differences in reading performance would disappear; PISA does not measure cause and effect. Transferring pupils who do badly may be partly a symptom, rather than a cause, of schools and school systems that are not producing satisfactory results, especially for lower-achieving students. It is worth noting that the schools with lower transfer rates tend to have greater autonomy and other means of addressing these challenges. The cluster of results listed above suggests that, in general, school systems that seek to cater to different students' needs through a high level of differentiation in the institutions, grade levels, and classes have not succeeded in producing superior overall results, and in some respects they have lower-than-average and more socially unequal performance.

Most successful school systems grant greater autonomy to individual schools to design curricula and establish assessment policies, but these school systems do not necessarily allow schools to compete for enrolment. The incentive to deliver good results for all students is not just a matter of how a school's student body is defined. It also depends on the ways in which schools are held accountable for their results and what forms of autonomy they are allowed to have—and how that could help influence their performance. PISA has looked at accountability both in terms of the information that is made available about performance and in terms of the use made of that information—whether by administrative authorities through rewards or control systems or by parents, for example through their choice of school. Thus, the issues of autonomy, evaluation, governance, and choice interact in providing a framework in which schools are given the incentives and the capacity to improve. PISA 2009 finds that:

- In countries where schools have greater autonomy over what is taught and how students are assessed, students tend to perform better.
- Within countries where schools are held to account for their results through posting achievement data publicly, schools that enjoy greater autonomy in resource allocation tend to do better than those with less autonomy. However, in countries where there are no such accountability arrangements, the reverse is true.
- Countries that create a more competitive environment in which many schools compete for students do not systematically produce better results.
- Within many countries, schools that compete more for students tend to have higher performance, but this is often accounted for by the higher socioeconomic status of students in these schools. Parents with a higher socio-economic status are more likely to take academic performance into consideration when choosing schools.
- In countries that use standards-based external examinations, students tend to do better overall, but there is no clear relationship

between performance and the use of standardized tests or the public posting of results at the school level. However, performance differences between schools with students of different social backgrounds are, on average, lower in countries that use standardized tests. (OECD, 2010, pp. 15–16)

After accounting for the socioeconomic and demographic profiles of students and schools, students in OECD countries who attend private schools show performance that is similar to that of students enrolled in public schools. On average, socioeconomically disadvantaged parents are over 13 percentage points more likely than socioeconomically advantaged parents to report that they consider low expenses and financial aid as very important determinants in choosing a school. If children from socioeconomically disadvantaged backgrounds cannot attend high-performing schools because of financial constraints, then school systems that offer parents more choice of schools for their children will necessarily be less effective in improving the performance of all students.

School systems considered successful tend to prioritize teachers' pay over smaller classes.

School systems differ in the amount of time, human, material and financial resources they invest in education. Equally important, school systems also vary in how these resources are spent:

- At the level of the school system and net of the level of national income, PISA shows that higher teachers' salaries, but not smaller class sizes, are associated with better student performance. Teachers' salaries are related to class size in that if spending levels are similar, school systems often make trade-offs between smaller classes and higher salaries for teachers. The findings from PISA suggest that systems prioritizing higher teachers' salaries over smaller classes tend to perform better, which corresponds with research showing that raising teacher quality is a more effective route to improved student outcomes than creating smaller classes.
- Within countries, schools with better resources tend to do better only to the extent that they also tend to have more socioeconomically advantaged students. Some countries show a strong relationship between schools' resources and their socioeconomic and demographic background, which indicates that resources are inequitably distributed according to schools' socioeconomic and demographic profiles.
- In other respects, the overall lack of a relationship between resources and outcomes does not show that resources are not important but that their level does not have a systematic impact within the prevailing range. If most or all schools have the minimum resource requirements to allow effective teaching, additional material resources may make little difference to outcomes.

There are still unanswered questions and concerns about implementing LRE, differentiating instruction, and meeting student needs within confines of policy and the commitment to best practices. When attempting to answer these and other questions, one needs to consider the professional debate and the education of students who are gifted, general education, and special educations. The ongoing debate continues to ensure educators are meeting student needs, common standards, common goals, and the law. The field of education has to navigate through all of these realities to offer an education to its population for now and for the future.

REFERENCES

Annenberg Institute. (2004). *Professional learning communities: Professional development strategies that improve instruction.* Providence, RI: Annenberg Institute.

Banks, J. A. (2001). *Cultural diversity and education: Foundations, curriculum, and teaching.* Boston: Allyn and Bacon.

Beninghof, A., & Singer, A. T. (1995). *Ideas for inclusion: The school administrator's guide.* Longmont, CO: Sopris West.

Burello, L. C., Schrup, M. G., & Barnett, B. G. (1998). *The principal as the special education instructional leader.* Presented at the Annual Convention of the Council for Exceptional Children. Washington, DC.

Byrnes, M. (1990). The regular education initiative debate: A review from the field. *Exceptional Children, 56*(4), 71–77.

Campbell, P., & Shaw, S. F. (1993). A process for systemic change: Planning for special education in the 21st century. *CASE in Point, 7*(2), 47–52.

Carlberg, C., & Kavale, K. (1980). The efficacy of special versus regular class placement for exceptional children: A meta-analysis. *Journal of Special Education, 14*(3) 295–309.

Choates, R. D. (1989). *Successful mainstreaming: Proven ways to detect and correct special needs.* Boston: Allyn & Bacon.

Council of Chief State School Officers (CCSSO). (1996). *Interstate School Leaders Licensure Consortium: Standards for School Leaders.* Washington, DC: CCSSO.

D'Alonzo, B., Giordano, G., & Cross, T. (1996). Improving teachers' attitudes through teacher education toward the inclusion of students with disabilities into their classrooms. *Teacher Educator, 31*(4), 304–312.

Darling-Hammond, L. (1997). *The right to learn.* San Francisco: Jossey-Bass.

Darling-Hammond, L., Ancess, J., & Ort, S. W. (2002). Reinventing high school: Outcomes of the coalition campus school project. *American Educational Research Journal, 39*(3), 639–673.

Darling-Hammond, L., Meyerson, D., LaPointe, M. M., & Orr, M. T. (2009). *Preparing principals for a changing world.* San Francisco, CA: Jossey-Bass.

Davis, S., Darling-Hammond, L., LaPointe, M., & Meyerson, D. (2005). *School leadership study developing successful principals.* Stanford: Stanford Educational Leadership Institute.

Davis, J., & Jazzar, M. (2005). The seven habits of effective principal preparation programs. *NAESP: Training Tomorrow's Principals, 84*(5), 18–21.

DuFour, R. and Eaker, R. (1998). *Professional learning communities at work: Best practices for enhancing student achievement.* Bloomington, IL: Solution Tree.

Echevarria, J., Vogt, M. E., & Short, D. (2004). *Making content comprehensible for English language learners: The SIOP model.* Boston: Allyn & Bacon.

Elliott, B., & Riddle, M. (1992). An effective interface between regular & special education: A synopsis of issues and successful practices. CASE Information Dissemination Packet. (ERIC Document Reproduction Service No. 358 650).

Ferri, B. A., & Connor, D. J. (2006). *Discourses of Exclusion in Desegregation and Inclusion Debates*. New York, Bern, Berlin, Bruxelles, Frankfurt am Main, Oxford, Wien, 2006. XII, 244 pp.

Friend, M., & Cook, L. (2007). *Interactions: Collaboration skills for school professionals*. Boston: Pearson.

Fritz, M. F., & Miller, M. (1995). Challenges of the inclusive classroom: Roles and responsibilities. *Contemporary Education, 66*(4), 211–214.

Fuchs, D., & Fuchs, L. S. (1994). Inclusive schools movement and the radicalization of special education reform. *Exceptional Children, 60*, 294–309.

Gardner, H. (2006). *Multiple intelligences: New horizons in theory and practice*. New York: Basic Books.

Garvar-Pinhas, A., & Schmelkin, L. P. (1989). Administrators' and teaches attitudes toward mainstreaming. *Remedial and Special Education, 10*, 38–43.

Goor, M., Schwenn, J. O., & Boyer, L. (1997). Preparing principals for leadership in special education. *Intervention in School and Clinic, 32*(3), 133–141.

Guskey, T. R. (Ed.). (2008). *Practical solutions for serious problems in standards-based grading*. Thousand Oaks, CA: Corwin Press.

Hesse-Biber, S., & Leavey, P. (2002). *The practice of qualitative research*. San Francisco CA: Sage.

Hulett, K. E. (2009). *Legal aspects of special education*. New Jersey: Pearson Education, Inc.

Ingersoll, R. (2003). *Is there really a teacher shortage?* Philadelphia: Consortium for Policy Research in Education, University of Pennsylvania.

Jacob, B. A., & Lefgren, L. (2002, April). *The impact of teacher training on student achievement: Quasi-experimental evidence from school reform efforts in Chicago*. National Bureau of Economic Research Working Paper 8916. Cambridge, MA: National Bureau of Economic Research.

Kruger, L. J., Struzziero, J., Watts, J., Vacca, D. (1995). The relationship between organizational support and satisfaction with teacher assistance teams. *Remedial and Special Educational, 16*(4), 203–211.

Leana, C. (2011). The Missing Link in School Reform. *Stanford Social Innovation Review*, Fall. Retrieved from http://www.ssireview.org/articles/entry/the_missing_link_in_school_reform.

Levine, A. (2005). *Educating school leaders*. New York: The Education School Project.

Lewis, A. (1994). *The inclusion of differently abled student in the regular classroom*. Reports/research/technical/speeches/conference papers. Retrieved October 30, 2006, from EDRS database.

Lombardi, T. P. (1994). *Responsible inclusion of students disabilities: Fastback 373*. Bloomington, IN: Phi Delta Kappa Educational Foundation.

Maras, P., & Brown, R. (1996). Effects of contact on children's attitudes toward disability: A longitudinal study. *Journal of Applied Social Psychology, 26*, 2113–2134.

Miles, K. H., Odden, A., Fermanich, M., & Archibald, S. (2004). Inside the black box of school district spending on professional development: Lessons from comparing jive urban districts. *Journal of Education Finance, 30*(1), 1–26.

Mostert, M. P., & Crockett, J. B. (1999–2000). Reclaiming the history of special education for more effective practice. *Exceptionality, 8*, 133–143.

Murphy, J. (1992). *The landscape of leadership preparation: Reframing the education of school*. San Francisco, CA: Corwin Press.

Murphy, J. (2001). The changing face of leadership preparation. *School Administrator 58*(10), 14–17.

Murphy, J. (2005). Unpacking the foundations of ISLLC standards and addressing concerns in the academic community. *Educational Administration Quarterly, 41*(91), 154–191.

Myles, B. S., & Simpson, R. L. (1989). Regular educators' modification preferences for mainstreaming mildly handicapped children, *Journal of Special Education, 22*, 479–491.

NASBE. (1992). *Winning ways: Creating inclusive schools, classrooms, and communities.* Alexandria, Virginia: ASCD.

National Center for Education Statistics (NCES). (1998). *Parent involvement in children's education: Efforts by public elementary schools.* Washington, DC: NCES.

National Center for Education Statistics (NCES). (2006). *School and parent interaction by household and poverty status:* 2002–03. Washington, DC: NCES.

National Center for Education Statistics (NCES). (2007). *The condition of education, 2007.* Washington, DC: NCES.

National Council for Accreditation of Teacher Education. (2000). *Program standards for elementary teacher preparation* and *professional standards for unit accreditation.* Washington, DC: NCATE.

National Policy Board for Educational Administration. (2001). *Recognizing and encouraging exemplary leadership in America's schools: A proposal to establish a system of advanced certification for administrators.* Washington, DC.

National Staff Development Council (NSDC). (2001). *NSDC's standards for staff development.* Oxford, OH: NSDC.

Orkwis, R. (1999). *Curriculum access and universal design for learning.* Arlington, VA: ERIC Clearinghouse on Disabilities and Gifted Children.

Organisation for Economic Cooperation and Development (OECD). (2010). Programme for International Student Assessment (PISA) 2009 Results: Executive Summary. Retrieved from http://www.oecd.org/pisa/pisaproducts/46619703.pdf.

Orr, M. T. (2003, April). *Evaluating educational leadership preparation: A review of empirical, conceptual and methodological literature.* Paper presented at the annual meeting of the American Educational Research Association. Chicago.

Orr, M. (2006). Mapping innovation in leadership preparation on our nation's schools of education. *Phi Delta Kappa,* vol. 87, no. 7, March, 492–499.

Pullan, M. (1991). *The new meaning of educational change.* New York: Teachers College Press.

Rogers, J. H., & Saklofske, D. H. (1985). Self-concepts, locus of control and performance expectations of learning disabled children. *Journal of Learning Disabilities,* May 1985, vol. 18, no. 5, 273–278.

Sage, D. D., & Burello, L. (1994). *Leadership in educational reform: An administrator's guide to changes in special education.* Baltimore: Paul Brookes.

Serpell, Z., & Bozeman, L. (1999). *Beginning teacher induction: A report on beginning teacher effectiveness and retention.* Washington, DC: National Partnership for Excellence and Accountability in Teaching.

Shanker, A. (1995). The Inclusive School: Full Inclusion Is Neither Free Nor Appropriate. *Educational Leadership.* Volume 52. Number 4. Pages 18–21.

Shanker, A. (1996). Where we stand on the rush to inclusion. American Federation of Teachers Speech given at AFT Conference on Full Inclusion Sheraton Washington Hotel, Washington, DC.

Strong, M., Fletcher, S., & Villar, A. (2004). *An investigation of the effects of teacher experience and teacher preparedness on the performance of Latino students in California.* Santa Cruz, CA: New Teacher Center.

State Consortium on Education Leadership. (2008). *An ISLLC-based guide to implementing leader standards and a companion guide to the educational leadership policy standards: ISLLC 2008. Performance expectation and indicators for education leaders.* Washington, DC: Council of Chief State School Officers.

"To the Best of Their Abilities," *Teacher Magazine,* 1995.

Tomlinson, C. A. (1999). *The differentiated classroom: Responding to the needs of all learners.* Alexandria, VA: ASCD.

Tomlinson, C.A. (2001). Standards and the art of teaching: Crafting high-quality classrooms. *NASSP Bulletin,* 85(22), 38–47

Trump, G. C., & Hange, J. E. (1996). *Concerns about, and effective teaching strategies for inclusion: focus Group interview findings from West Virginia Teachers.* Charleston, West

Virginia: Appalachia Educational laboratory. ERIC Document Reproduction Service no. ED 397578.

U.S. Census Bureau. (2009). *Statistical abstract of the United States: 2008* (127th ed.). Washington, DC: U.S. Census Bureau.

U.S. Department of Education. (2004). *Amendments to the Individuals with Disabilities Educations Act (IDEA).* Washington DC: U.S. Department of Education.

U.S. Department of Education. (2007a). *The condition of education, 2007.* Washington, DC: U.S. Department of Education.

U.S. Department of Education. (2007b). *Twenty-seventh annual report to Congress on the implementations of the Individual with Disabilities Act.* Washington, DC: U.S. Department of Education.

U.S. Department of Education. (2009). *Twenty-eighth annual report to Congress on the implementation of the Individuals with Disabilities Education Act, 2006,* vol. 1. Washington, DC: U.S. Department of Education.

Van Drenth, L., Gabel, S., & Danforth, S. (2005). Disability and the Politics of Education *An International Reader Forward.*

Voltz, D. L. (2003). Personalized contextual instruction. *Preventing School Failure, 47,* 138–143.

Voltz, D. L. (2006). Inclusion in an era of accountability: A framework for differentiating instruction in urban standards-based classrooms. *Journal of Urban Learning, Teaching, and Research, 2,* 95–105.

Voltz, D. L., Sims M. J., & Nelson, B. (2010). *Connecting teachers students and standards: Strategies for success in diverse and inclusive classrooms.* Alexandria, VA: ASCD.

Wagner, M., Levine, P., Blackerby, J., & Knokey, A. M. (2007). Relationships between the schools program of students with disabilities and their longitudinal outcomes. In J. Blackorby, A. W. Knokey, M. Wagner, P. Levine, E. Schiller, C. Sumi, *What makes a difference? Influences on outcomes for student with disabilities* (pp. 3-1–3-13). Menlo Park, CA: SRI International. Retrieved from http://www.seels.net/design-docs/SEELS_W1W3_FINAL.pdf.

Waldron, N. L., & McLeskey, J. (1998). The effects of an inclusive school program on students with mild and severe learning disabilities, *Exceptional Children, 64,* 395–405.

Whittier, K. S., & Hewitt, J. S. (1993). Intervention in School and Clinic, 29(2), 84–88.

Wilmore, E. (2002). *Principal leadership, applying the new Educational Leadership Constituent Council (ELCC) standards.* Thousand Oaks, CA: Corwin Press.

SEVEN

Differentiation: Does It Really Work?

Kathryn F. Accurso

University education programs promote and prescribe pedagogical practices that embrace "differentiated" teaching and learning. Differentiated learning requires teachers to adjust their lesson plans to meet the individual potentials and learning styles of students in the classroom. The objective for differentiated instruction cannot be argued with. Its positive goal is lofty but too often unrealistic. Preparing lesson strategies, content, and implementation for all learners presupposes that remediation for slower learners, content support for average, and enrichment for above average can be met in a prescribed period of time.

Students who are at the average and above average range need maturity to work independently and often have difficulty adjusting to flexible teaching schedules. Thus, while the concept of differentiation seems doable, reality oftentimes presents a different story for the average and above average students in an inclusive classroom.

WHAT IS DIFFERENTIATION?

Differentiating instruction means changing the pace, level, or kind of instruction you provide in response to individual learners' needs, styles, or interests. Differentiated instruction specifically responds to students' progress on the learning continuum—what they already know and what they need to learn. It responds to their best ways of learning and allows them to demonstrate what they've learned in ways that capitalize on their strengths and interests (Heacox, 2001).

Differentiation means tailoring instruction to meet individual needs. Whether teachers differentiate content, processes, products, or the learning environment, the use of ongoing assessment and flexible grouping makes this a successful approach to instruction. At its most basic level, differentiation consists of the efforts of teachers to respond to variance among learners in the classroom. Whenever a teacher reaches out to an individual or small group to vary his or her teaching in order to create the best learning experience possible, that teacher is differentiating instruction (Tomlinson, 2000, np).

My daughter convinced me to try a new class at the gym we belong to. As the class started, I waited for the instructor to explain how the moves could be modified for those of us who needed to modify them. She never did, so I did the best I could, knowing the limitations of my left knee. As the class went on, it became more and more difficult for me to keep up, even though I was trying to modify the moves to meet my abilities. It wasn't long before I realized that I was in over my head and the instructor had no idea how to accommodate anyone other than those who could fully participate in her class. I walked out of the class after a half hour, frustrated that the instructor had not had the insight to address the needs of all the participants in her class.

As I thought about this experience, I realized that this must be how our students feel in the classroom. But, the thing is, our students can't walk out of the classroom when they become frustrated. In today's classroom, where the student's abilities often fall from below grade level to above grade level and everywhere in between, it is the teacher's responsibility to make sure that every student in the is able to learn at a pace that is comfortable for them. Not every student will have had the same experiences or be from the same cultural or socioeconomic background. Students who come to school not speaking English sit side by side with gifted students. Yet we develop one lesson plan that includes them all.

Differentiation is a way of meeting each student where they are, addressing their needs, and helping them to reach their full potential. How can we do this in a class of twenty-four plus students?

All teachers have experienced introducing a new concept to their students only to realize that some of the students have already mastered the skill and are able to apply it, while other students "don't get it." Changing our plans as we go in order to reach all students is a good teaching practice, but it is not differentiating. Many teachers lack a clear understanding of differentiated instruction, mistakenly implementing only surface-level strategies in the classroom. Differentiating means knowing your students' strengths and preparing a lesson that offers variations in content, process, and product to meet the needs of all students.

Far too often the classroom teacher addresses the needs of the struggling students by either reteaching the lesson, teaching the lesson in a different way, or asking the struggling students to do less work than their peers. What about the average and above average student in that same classroom who do understand the lesson the first time it is taught? How is the lesson being differentiated to meet their needs? These students need lessons that are going to challenge and engage them, not just be handed more work to do as is often the case.

In differentiated classrooms, teachers begin where students are, not at the front of the curriculum guide. They accept and build on the premise that learners differ in important ways. In differentiated classrooms, teachers ensure that a student competes with himself as he grows and develops rather than with other students (Tomlinson, 1999, np).

After assessing the student's areas of strengths, interests, and learning style, the teacher should examine the content, process and product to determine how each of these areas can be differentiated to reach the maximum number of students. Teachers may differentiate any one, two, or all three areas depending on the circumstances.

Differentiated instruction requires proactive planning rather than re-active teaching. Knowing the students strengths, readiness levels, learning styles, interests, and areas of weakness allows the teacher to develop a plan that helps each student learn new information in a way that best meets their styles, readiness levels, and interests. While all students need to get to the finish line, how and when they get there may be different for each student.

Dr. Hall (2002) states:

> To differentiate instruction is to recognize students' varying background knowledge, readiness, language, preferences in learning, and interests, and to react responsively. Differentiated instruction is a process to approach teaching and learning for students of differing abilities in the same class. The intent of differentiating instruction is to maximize each student's growth and individual success by meeting each student where he or she is, and assisting in the learning process. (np)

Content—or what the students learn—is often dictated by a prepared curriculum that is often geared toward the average student in that particular grade level. Content can be differentiated by providing materials on a variety of levels in the same classroom. Having reading materials that address the content to be taught on varied levels is just one of the ways to differentiate instruction. Varying the levels of difficulty when presenting content materials offers students the opportunity to start at their present knowledge and proceed at their own pace. This means that those students who already have an understanding of the content do not have to sit through a lesson they already know but, rather, can participate in enrichment activities or learning centers to deepen their knowledge. Students who are having trouble grasping the concept, however, are af-forded time to learn it before moving on. The class does not necessarily move through the curriculum as a whole but rather at pace that allows the students the benefit of time and individuality. This all sounds wonderful on paper, but in reality it is not quite so easy. For most students this would require working independently or in small groups. Few students have the maturity to do this, especially elementary school students. This takes appropriate training and adult supervision to be successful. A common complaint of teachers is that there is not sufficient planning time needed on a daily and weekly basis to deal effectively with the management of differentiation in their classrooms.

The process—or how the students make sense and learn the information in a lesson—can be differentiated by learning style, student interest, or readiness skills. The process can also be adjusted by using a variety of methods to present the content, such as lectures, peer teaching, videos, music, books, and manipulatives. Students can work independently, in small groups or with the teacher. Differentiating by process refers to how a student comes to understand and assimilate facts, concepts, and skills (Anderson, 2007).

Differentiating the product allows the student a choice in how they will demonstrate what they have learned. Students can use typical assessments or more individualized approaches such as multimedia presentations, poetry, photography, bulletin boards, or editorials, to name a few. The students demonstrate that they have met the learning outcomes using their particular strengths and interests. Many believe that the varied work products extend learning beyond the four walls of the classroom and help to motivate all students.

WHAT DIFFERENTIATION ISN'T

Individualized Instruction

Differentiation is not individualized instruction. Individualized instruction is instruction that personalizes the lesson in the classroom to meet the diverse needs of the students. This is done in several ways. First, the pace of instruction is varied for students. Once a skill is mastered, the student can move on to the next skill and not be held back by waiting for the rest of the students to catch up. Likewise, students who require more time on a particular topic are afforded it, without worry that the rest of the class has moved on. In an individualized instructional classroom, students move through the curriculum at their own pace. A student may move through the science curriculum rather quickly, as this is an area of interest or strength, yet move much more slowly through the math curriculum, as this requires more effort from this particular student. This can mean that students are at various levels in different subjects as well.

Second, teachers adjust the method of instruction to accommodate the learning styles of the students. There is reduced lecture time and more time spent on self-paced, self-corrective work. Students who work best in small groups can do so, while those who prefer to work independently do just that. Individualized instruction came into focus between 1910 and 1920. Although individualized instruction does offer an alternative to traditional instruction, these plans were not very successful, probably because of the herculean task of developing and managing individualized lesson plans for upward of twenty students at a time.

Tracking

Differentiated instruction should not be confused with tracking. Tracking is the grouping of students according to their academic abilities. Tracking or ability grouping was originally instituted as a way of meeting the needs of all students. Many would argue that tracking is unfair to the students, for students who are placed in the low track rarely move through the system to a higher ability level. Students placed in the low-ability track move through the curriculum more slowly than those placed in the higher-ability groups, who are at times required to move rapidly through the curriculum.

It is believed that students in different tracks do not receive the same quality of education as those students not placed in academic tracks. What was thought to be a way of improving academic achievement for all students, including the special education students, quickly became a way of segregating students into the "haves and have nots." Gamoran (1987) found that the achievement gap between low- and high-track students was larger than the gap between students who leave high school without graduating and high school graduates. He also found that low-income students and students of color were disproportionately represented in lower tracks.

As inclusion of special education students and English language learners has become the norm in more and more classrooms as educators have rethought tracking and look toward a more heterogeneous setting that offers quality educational opportunities to all students.

Failing Scores on State Tests

Under No Child Left Behind (2001), the United States has been assessing students in third through eighth grade in reading and mathematics in order to measure their yearly academic progress. Although an effort has been made to reduce the achievement gap in reading and mathematics, learning gaps in these areas still exists. The Common Core State Standards and the new, more rigorous state assessments have many teachers in fear that a differentiated approach to learning will hinder the student's

performance on the state test. "Why should I differentiate in my classroom when all students are required to take the same state test in the
spring?" one third-grade teacher asks (in a personal interview). Differentiating instruction does not mean a teacher is changing the curriculum or
"dumbing it down." The goal of differentiating is to offer students the
opportunity to learn in an environment that is conducive to their learning
style, interests, and at a pace that is comfortable for them. If the students
know the material, they will do well on the state assessment, regardless
of how they acquired the knowledge.

Test-taking strategies have their place in a differentiated classroom;
these are skills the students will need in many areas of their lives. Teaching students how to approach materials and activities such as tests and
assessments that are not differentiated is also part of the curriculum in a
differentiated classroom. Students in a differentiated classroom have the
same advantage taking the state assessments as the students from a more
traditional classroom.

Small Group Instruction

Another misconception about differentiated instruction is that it consists solely of small-group instruction, eliminating whole-group instruction. Actually, in a differentiated classroom, the instruction is delivered
in several ways, including whole group, small group and individualized.
The teacher may change the mode of instruction daily depending on the
students' strengths and the learning outcomes for a particular lesson.
Teachers in differentiated classrooms must be keenly aware of the students' interests and areas, where the students excel, as well as areas and
subjects that the students are not as familiar or comfortable with. Teachers work to develop a plan of action that allows each student to work
toward his or her personal best using his or her strengths and weakness.
The teacher is constantly asking the students to build on what they know
and to stretch themselves beyond their comfort zone—to broaden their
knowledge.

Changing the Quantity of Work

In a differentiated classroom where students with individualized education plans (IEP), gifted and talented students, and average students all
learn together, some accommodations must be made to ensure that all
students' needs are being met. Teachers who have not had the proper
professional development or teacher training mistakenly think that giving the special needs students less work or the gifted and talented students more work is "differentiated." But, of course, this is not what differentiation is about. Many educators are outside their comfort zone in
modifying curriculum, as such work requires additional knowledge and

skills teachers may not have. Teachers are further challenged by students who are exceptional in more than one area (twice or thrice exceptional), (VanTassel-Baska & Stambaugh, 2005).

Although we need to look at the curriculum—and how it is delivered to the students—merely giving less or more work will not address the needs of students. In fact, it is not unusual to find that many of the students reading to learn in a classroom are not reading on grade level. How, then, are these students going to acquire the knowledge necessary to be successful if they cannot read the text? Oftentimes, the teacher will read the text to these students in an effort to help and differentiate the instruction. These are the very students who should be reading more to improve their skills, yet they are the ones being read to. Cunningham and Stanovich (1998) tell us that

> an early start in reading is important in predicting a lifetime of literacy experience—and this is true regardless of the level of reading comprehension ability that the individual eventually attains. They go on to say that the very act of reading can help children compensate for modest levels of cognitive ability by building their vocabulary and general knowledge. In other words, ability is not the only variable that counts in the development of intellectual functioning. Those who read a lot will enhance their verbal intelligence; that is, reading will make them smarter. (p. 7)

CAN DIFFERENTIATION WORK?

How do we reach all students in a classroom where we have such diverse learners? It's imperative that administration and teachers work side by side to develop their own definition of and philosophy for implementing differentiation in their school.

The diversity of students in today's classrooms exemplifies the need to teach in such a way that we are maximizing learning for all students. In an effort to find a way to educate all our students, many educators have begun to look at differentiated instruction. Although this approach is not new—in fact, it has been used for years to teach the gifted and special education students—many are just now beginning to realize its potential in reaching students with various readiness levels, interests, and learning styles. The more teachers learn about their students, the more they are able to design effective experiences that elicit real learning (Edwards, Carr, & Siegel, 2006).

The differentiated classroom aims to provide special education students with mild to moderate learning disabilities a meaningful learning experience alongside their average and above average classmates. The special education students may have the intellectual ability to master the curriculum but have not met with success because of their learning disabilities. In a differentiated setting, the content, process, and product are varied to meet all students' interest and abilities. Lawrence-Brown (2004) confirms that differentiated instruction can enable students with a wide range of abilities—from gifted students to those with mild or even severe disabilities—to receive an appropriate education in inclusive classrooms. The teacher may use the information and recommendations made on the student's IEP, surveys, student interviews, and classroom observations, along with informal conversations with the student to gain insight into his or her interests, strengths, and weaknesses. This will help the teacher to place the students in the appropriate instructional groups. Although the assignments are tiered in this differentiated classroom, some assignments may need to be modified for the special education students. Classroom teachers can consult with their special education colleagues to establish what assignments are appropriate for these students. Unfortunately, few schools still have teachers for the gifted and talented, which leaves the classroom teacher to provide for these students. Many teachers are not well versed in taking a lesson and differentiating it in such a way as to meet the needs of the struggling learner while also addressing the average and above average students' learning needs.

Differentiation takes the philosophy of inclusion a step further to provide for the individual needs of all students within a general education classroom. Differentiation describes a philosophy that seeks to make education more meaningful for all students, from high-achieving, gifted students to those who are struggling in school (Tomlinson, 1999, np).

If schools are to be successful in the implementation of differentiated classrooms, they must provide the teachers with the needed professional development and mentors.

It is easy to see how some educators would think that differentiated instruction and inclusive education go hand in hand. However, there are many things to consider when looking to instruct special education students in the differentiated classroom. First, it is important to be certain that the level of instruction is appropriate to the student's readiness level. In a differentiated classroom, assignments are geared toward the student's ability. However, a special education student may need more support than a general education student in completing a task or producing a product. Second, the nature of the student's disability must be taken into consideration when placing the student in any setting. A differentiated classroom that does not have the appropriate support of an aide or paraprofessional may not be the setting for a student with a behavior disorder who needs frequent breaks outside the classroom. Last, not all general education teachers have the expertise working with students with disabilities. These teachers may need to consult with the special education specialist in the building for support. According to Barton (2003), factors that affect overall student achievement include the rigor of the curriculum; the experience, quality, and commitment of the teachers; the learning environment, including safety and expectations of students; and class size.

A successful differentiated classroom requires students to work independently. In a differentiated classroom, this may mean spending instructional time to teach students the independent strategies necessary to be successful in this setting. Students with an IEP may need additional support for learning to work independently. The role of the teacher in the differentiated classroom is very different from that of the teacher in the traditional classroom. While there is some whole-group instruction, much of the work is done in smaller groups or individually. In order to manage the many different activities that are going on simultaneously, the teacher must be aware of the student's readiness levels, interests, and learning styles. Collaboration between the general and special educators, support staff (such as reading and math specialists), as well as any appropriate service providers help to make this a rewarding learning experience for all the students. Of course, what works today may not work the following year; as your population changes, so must the classroom expectations, activities, and teaching.

Today when many schools are looking for ways to reintroduce the special education population back into the mainstream, it is important to keep in mind that the needs of the average and above average students also be met in the differentiated classroom. I'm reminded of the old adage, "The squeaky wheel gets the grease." Many times our average and above average students are not so squeaky, and as a result, their needs may go unmet. They need to be engaged and challenged to work to their personal best. All students have a right to an education that encourages them to practice higher-level critical thinking skills and allows them to participate in meaningful learning experiences in a classroom that is student centered.

Each year in my second-grade class, we are learning about memoirs. During this lesson, we do an author study on my favorite children's author, Tomie dePaola. As I read his book *The Art Lesson* (1997) to my students, I can't help but think about how much has changed in education since Tomie went to school. In the story, Tomie talks about wanting to use his box of sixty-four crayons that he received for his birthday. His teacher tells him he must use the school-issued box of eight crayons because everyone must use the same crayons, otherwise it wouldn't be fair to the others. A differentiated classroom is just about as far from Tomie's experience as you can get. As I read the story and shake my head at the rigidity of the teacher, I also recognize that there are still teachers like the one in his story. They are unable to differentiate for the gifted students, forcing them to sit through lessons on material that they already know because it wouldn't be fair to let them do something different. For a differentiated classroom to truly work, all participants must understand something my college professor told me many years ago:

"Fair means that everybody gets what everybody needs, not that everybody gets the same thing."

The practice of changing a school's approach to teaching is comprehensive. It involves efforts by teachers, administrators, parents, and community members over a given period of time and demands attention to every component of the school day and curriculum. In looking at differentiated instruction as a way to reduce remediation, reach more of the students on a level that is comfortable for them, and include special education students into the general education classrooms, the school must be willing to rethink its current model of teaching and learning. Successful school improvement requires that all stakeholders share the same vision for their school and students. This work cannot be completed quickly or without the proper professional development needed for all those involved. Knapp (1997) notes that the engagement of teachers in professional communities is important in implementing any reform.

Throughout the process, teachers need to rely heavily on the data collected from assessments, both formal and informal, as well as any alternative assessments that may use in the differentiated classroom. This data will help teachers and administrators to follow the student's progress and to make any necessary adjustments in either the curriculum or the delivery.

Change is difficult. Changing the way a school looks at its teaching practices and how their students learn is a task that requires teamwork, patience, and a belief in the vision as they stumble through the process. Those who believe in the process will help those who are not able to see the end result as clearly. Knowing that the school has worked together to provide their students with a quality education, one in which the students are active participants, will give the teachers and administrators great pride.

For all its promise, effective differentiation is complex to use and, thus, difficult to promote in schools. Moving toward differentiation is a long-term change process. It is best to begin by seeking out the wisdom of other educators who have experience with differentiated instruction, ground your own practice in the theory, and learn in a way that is meaningful to you (Tomlinson, 1999, np).

REFERENCES

Anderson, K. M. (2007). Differentiating instruction to include all students. *Preventing School Failure, 51*(3), 49–54.

Barton, P. E. (2003). Parsing the achievement gap: Baselines for tracking progress. Princeton, NJ: Educational Testing Service.

Cunningham, A., & Stanovich, K. (1998). What reading does for the mind. *American Educator*, vol. 22, no. 1–2, pp. 8–15.

DePaola, T. (1997). *The art lesson.* New York: Penguin USA.

Edwards, C. J., Carr, S., & Siegel, W. (2006). Influences of experiences and training on effective teaching practices to meet the needs of diverse learners in schools. *Education, 126*(3), 580–592.

Gagne, R. M., Briggs, L. J., & Wager, W. W. (1992). *Principles of instructional design.* Fort Worth, TX: Harcourt Brace Jovanovich College.

Gamoran, A. (1987). The stratification of high school learning opportunities. *Sociology of Education, 60,* 135–155.

Hall, T. (2002). *Differentiated instruction.* Wakefield, MA: CAST. Retrieved from www.cast.org/publications/ncac/ncac_diffinstruc.html.

Heacox, D. (2001). *Differentiating instruction in the regular classroom: How to reach and teach all learners, grades 3–12.* Free Spirit Publishing.

Knapp, M. (1997). Between systemic reforms and the mathematics and science classroom: The dynamics of innovation, implementation, and professional learning. *Review of Educational Research, 67*(2), 227–266.

Lawrence-Brown, D. (2004). Differentiated instruction: Inclusive strategies for standards-based learning that benefit the whole class. *American Secondary Education 32*(3), 34.

No Child Left Behind Act of 2001. Pub. L. No. 107–110, § 115 Stat. 1425.

Rubin, B. (2006). Tracking and detracking: Debates, evidence, and best practices for a heterogeneous world. *Theory into Practice, 45*(1), 4–14.

Tomlinson, C. A. (1999). *The differentiated classroom: Responding to the needs of all learners.* Alexandria, VA: ASCD. Retrieved from http://www.ascd.org/publications/books/199040.aspx.

Tomlinson, C. A. (2000, August). Differentiation of instruction in the elementary grades. *ERIC Digest.* Retrieved from http://ecap.crc.illinois.edu/eecearchive/digests/2000/tomlin00.pdf.

VanTassel-Baska, J., & Stambaugh, T. (2005). Challenges and possibilities for serving gifted learners in the regular classroom. *Theory into Practice, 44*(3), 211–217.

EIGHT

Outcomes for Mainstreamed, Full-inclusion, and Separate Classrooms

Janet D. Mulvey

Milliron (2012) writes,

> Education is the best tool to bring positive change to society, to develop a generation of responsible individuals and contribute to the development of good human beings. The fundamental purpose is to gain knowledge . . . to develop oneself physically, mentally and socially. (p. 4)

The question in this chapter is how do we provide the type of education to realize the full potential for our students, today and in the future? How do we comply with the legal mandates of the Special Education Law, support children with disabilities, and implement the best instruction possible to students in the regular classroom? Which model best suits all students: separate classrooms, mainstreaming, or full inclusion?

It is estimated that 60 percent of students with disabilities spend 80 percent of their time in the regular classroom setting (Deninger, 2008). Some are mainstreamed; they are placed in the regular education classroom but receive special support services outside, in either resource rooms or special classes. The fully included (inclusion) model places students with disabilities in the regular classroom 100 percent of the time. The separate classroom model places students with disabilities in a separate classroom with some inclusion in special areas (physical education, music, art, etc.).

This chapter will examine the outcomes for all students, in particular the average and above average students, in classrooms that can house up to 40 percent of students with disabilities. Legal mandates and advocates for those with special needs have successfully won the right for full inclusion for many students. Results for the regular, average student have been compromised, lowering standards and content knowledge and causing less engagement in learning.

STRUCTURE FOR SPECIAL EDUCATION CLASSES

Separate classrooms and schools have been reserved for the more severely disabled—physically, emotionally, and cognitively. Classes are small, teacher aides are assigned (sometimes one on one), and lessons are based on basic life skills. Funding for these schools is mainly based on state and local taxes, costing up to $67,000 per child per year. The amount of money spent, while necessary for severely disabled students, reduces the funding for students in regular classrooms.

Visiting a special education school, one will find more adults than children, classes with cognitively challenged children, and resources mandated to serve them. Teachers are trained to implement special programs with the goal of teaching the students self-care and survival skills. Funding needs, based on salaries for assistants, special equipment costs, and administration costs, are at an all-time high, detracting from the needs of the regular education students in our public schools.

Separate classrooms within the regular education public school setting allow students to move as a class from their special setting into the mainstream for content area instruction. The special education teacher moves with them to supply support in the regular classroom. This situation provides preparation in the content area prior to the regular classroom instruction and then reinforcement for understanding.

Mainstreaming is the process of including special education students in the regular classroom. One method involves selecting regular education classes or subject areas of strength for the student with disabilities. Students leave the special support classroom and "mainstream" into the regular education class. They then return to the special setting to receive for content areas in which they need special support or remediation. Other interpretations of mainstreaming are synonymous with inclusion, where students remain in the general education classroom for the entire day but where the special educator "pushes in" to give support.

Inclusion is the practice of including students with disabilities in the regular education program full time. Students do not leave for special remedial services; all must be provided in the inclusion of the regular education program. Several educational organizations advocate for all students with disabilities, even those with high incidence, to be educated within the general education setting.

Most educators in schools today are well aware of the mandates for special education in their schools. Legal mandates are cited and reinforced for compliance in every school in the nation. The application, however, varies according to the wealth of the district, the knowledge of the parents, and the ability to supply resources to the best advantage for the students.

Outcomes are based on all three factors mentioned above. The following examines the application of the law and the implementation factors affecting students in mainstreamed and inclusion classrooms. In a discussion about special education terms, the manifestation of the "place" where student are situated becomes a major issue. According to the Association for Persons with Severe Disabilities (1991), "students (regardless of their disability) should be educated in the general education classroom" (p. 2). Thus, where the students are literally placed becomes the same classroom as same-aged peers.

Our argument against a one-place-suits-all approach is based on the need for a continuum of placements based on the individual needs of the student. In addition, although there are no laws cited to provide a free and appropriate public education (FAPE) for the general education student, mandates to provide them with the most appropriate and best education possible are long overdue.

Positive results for special needs students in an all-inclusion class, while touted by advocates, are often based on wishes and hope. There have been some benefits socially, and, when supported by the addition of a full-time special education teacher in the classroom, some academic gains. In a study done by the Canadian Council on Learning (2009), mixed results and modest advantages provided by inclusion suggested a mere inclusive placement is no guarantee of success. The studies of initiatives where included students with special educational needs (SEN) were successful were characterized by adequate support and, beyond that, available to both general and special education students. Often this involved team teaching and/or extensive collaboration with a qualified special education teacher. Simply placing students with SEN in mainstream classrooms is no recipe for success. In addition, few studies report academic benefits to students with SEN.

COURT DECISIONS

Courts have been asked to adjudicate claims from parents that their child has been denied their due right under recently reorganized Individuals with Disabilities Education Act (IDEA, 2004). Rulings have differed, but some guidelines have been established that ask questions for consideration. These questions can serve to help deliver the best education possible for all students: general education and those with special needs:

1. To what extent must a school go to provide services?

2. What are the most important, academic, and social factors determining a placement?
3. What are the rights of the other children in the classroom?

The following case, adjudicated in favor of a student with disabilities, brings to question numbers 1 and 3: To what extent must a school district go to provide services? What rights do other children have in the classroom when courts mandate inclusion of special services for one child?

In *Kalbfleisch v. Columbia Community School District* (2009), parents of Carter Kalbfleisch, a five-year-old with autism, filed suit in Illinois state court, seeking an injunction to immediately compel the school district to permit their son to bring his service dog with him to his pre-K classroom. The parents claimed that the service dog made the student happier, reduced the length and frequency of tantrums, and was trained to take him down if he took off running into a dangerous situation. The school district denied the use of the service dog, as the student had successfully attended school in the past without the use of the service dog. There was a policy of no animals at the school, and there was another student with a rare lung disease who was highly allergic to dogs and had been told there would be no dogs at school. The case was first moved to federal court based on IDEA mandates but was moved back to state court. The Eighth District state court issued a preliminary injunction allowing the service dog in the school due to the fact the parents met the Illinois state statute standard under the Americans with Disabilities Act's (ADA) definition of a service dog.

The court cited no evidence that the school district could not accommodate the highly allergic student and the autistic child's request for the dog. It added there was no evidence the school district would suffer a great hardship by allowing the dog to accompany the child in school.

The case brings into question the rights of the "other" in the school. Does the right of the autistic child override the rights of the allergic general education child? Is there a double standard? Have we gone so far that we have forgotten the rights of those in regular education?

Courts have been inconsistent in their rulings, suggesting interpretation of the law is often based on misunderstanding of the rights of both students with special needs and those in the general education population. Inappropriate placement of students with special needs in a general education setting can result in unfair education for all students. Decisions made to comply with all demands from advocates for the student with special needs is inherently an impediment of the education rights of other students. According to Marissa Antoinette (2002):

> If the disabled student, with supplementary aides and services requires so much of the teacher's time that the teacher cannot give adequate attention to the needs of other students in the classroom, is so disruptive . . . that education of other students is impacted and/or requires the

curriculum to be significantly modified, the general education classroom may not be an appropriate setting for the student. (p. 2046)

In *Daniel R.R. v. State Board of Education* (1989), a six-year-old moderately
retarded boy with a developmental age between two and three was
mainstreamed into a regular education kindergarten class for half a day.
The teacher reported the young boy was not benefiting from the placement either academically or socially and was detracting from the needs of
the other kindergarteners. In this case, although the parents appealed
three times, the Fifth Circuit Court applied IDEA compliance standards:
Could regular education placement with supportive services provide
satisfactory achievement? Had the school mainstreamed the child to the
fullest extent?

The case in this instance took into account the benefits for all students,
including regular education and those with special needs, and ruled in
favor of the school (placing the student in a special class).

Parents, advocates, school districts and courts need to understand the
intent of IDEA, remove the political and emotional factors, and apply the
law to benefit of the student—all students.

Full inclusion, currently being advocated for all students, regardless
of their disability, is raising concern for educators and the assessments
tied to annual yearly progress. The recent poll taken by Gallup and reported in *Education Week* in 2012, cites the increase in student disengagement as they move from elementary to middle to high school. Brandon
Busteed (2012), Gallup's executive director, points out on the organization's blog, "The drop in student engagement for each year students are
in school is our monumental, collective failure" (np).

The practice of standardized testing as an indicator of success for
students and teachers in inclusive classrooms often results in "teaching to
the test." Engagement levels decline, learning becomes tedious, and boredom results in disconnection to the purpose of education. Students who
are ready to be challenged, excited, and motivated are, instead, treated to
a lackluster curriculum focused on passing a test along with their peers
with special needs.

The graph in figure 8.1 represents the drop in engagement from elementary to middle to high school. The survey covered 50,000 students in
37 states and 1,700 public schools. Representation of urban, suburban,
and rural schools showed little difference in percentage of engagement,
leaving us to question the objective of schooling for all students in the
United States.

OUTCOMES

How do we measure the benefits of placements for all students in the public school system? Are there winners and losers? Can we find a continuum where all are winners under the best circumstances possible?

Instead of focusing on the "place," we must emphasize students' potential outcomes commensurate with twenty-first century skills. Does the location matter, or is it how we implement proven pedagogical strategies that motivate and increase the quest for more?

The push for inclusion of all students into the general education setting has become more demanding by parents and advocates. Their purpose is to provide an educational and social environment inherent in the regular classroom. In the current standardized test environment where teacher evaluations are predicated on the results, the placement is detrimental to all, but specifically to the general education student. According to Hocutt (1996),

> There is no compelling evidence that placement rather than instruction is the critical factor in student academic or social success. Further, studies have indicated that typical practice in general education is substantially different from practice in the model programs that showed greatest success for students with disabilities. The interventions that were effective in improving academic outcomes for students with disabilities required a considerable investment of resources, including time and effort, as well as extensive support for teachers. (p. 77)

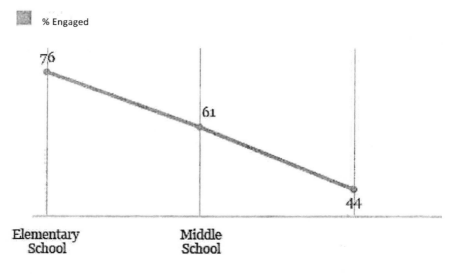

Figure 8.1.   The School Cliff: Students' Engagement Drops Over Time

Case Study 1

Kathy is a teacher in the New York City public schools, with both undergraduate and master's degree in education. She was interested in administrative leadership and began pursuing a second master's to become a school principal. Her passion for teaching and learning were apparent as she participated in the education leadership program.

The second year into her leadership program, her demeanor began to change, her weariness became apparent, and her lack of usual engagement slipped. Due to her strong performance in the high school social studies program, she was given a general education inclusion class. The makeup of the class consisted of 40 percent of students with IEPs. Without assistance, she was told to differentiate the lessons but to make sure all students passed the New York Social Studies Regents.

Kathy's passion for teaching and learning was replaced with tension, lack of confidence, and despair in not only being unprepared for the special needs of her IEP students, the loss of interest in the general education group, and the pressure from the administration to have all students pass the regents exam.

This is not a unique story in poorer-resourced districts across the country. Academic outcomes for students, in this and similar situations, are minimal at best and usually punitive for the teacher. The outcome for education, in general, was the loss of an effective teacher and a future school leader.

What would the situation looked like if place was not the criteria for the student but, instead, a program meeting the needs and potential for all? Integrating students with special needs into the regular education program can be accomplished with understanding and foresight. Expectations for all students to learn the same content and be tested within the "place" of the regular classroom is unfair for those with disabilities and, if the program is modified, unfair for the regular education student.

John Elder Robison, an author with Asperger's clearly states, "As the evidence for neurodiversity accumulates, it seems increasingly likely that an overall cure for neurological difference is not possible, and if diversity is at the root of certain people's achievements, it is not desirable either" (2013, np). If we are to take this authors personal experience and research into consideration, why are we subjecting our students with neurological differences to learning situations ineffective?

Case Study 2

In a suburban school in Westchester, the principal in the school, along with a special and a regular education teacher, developed a system to benefit the learning for a special class of twelve students and a regular education class of twenty. Both teachers worked together to develop the curriculum in literacy and social studies. An integrated curriculum allowed for historically written material (fiction and nonfiction) as the basis for teaching and learning in this sixth-grade classroom.

Prior to the lesson, the special education teacher pre-prepared her students in the special education classroom. Using strategies specific to their needs, the students were given the opportunity to enter the regular education classroom with prior knowledge and clear expectations for the content. The regular education teacher taught the entire class the pre-planned material without compromising content or delivery for the general education students. The special education teacher, in turn, reviewed what was taught with her students. Quizzes and exams demonstrated that all students had achieved a level of achievement, enjoyment, and engagement in the lessons.

All students in the special and regular education classes attended art, music, and physical education classes as one. The combination provided social opportunities for all, as well as a feeling of accomplishment for academic knowledge. A trained special education teacher provided students in the selfcontained special education class preteaching strategies, while the regular education students received content knowledge at grade level from a trained regular education professional.

Financial burdens placed on school districts due to the increase of costs and number of students identified with special needs have been a major factor in mainstreamed and inclusive placements. Full detail of these costs will be discussed in chapter 9, but suffice it to mention the state and federal governments have decreased their contribution, leaving the burden of cost to local schools. Figure 8.2 illustrates the unintended result for students in regular classroom where compliance for those with special needs is mandated and financial support is lacking. More special education in public schools without adequate resources places the burden on districts to comply with IDEA mandates. Compliance often means placements that affect the ability to give regular education students the rigor and challenges they need to succeed or remain engaged.

Parents, school personnel, and the courts must focus on the function of education; our national security depends on a productive, democratic, and socioeconomically independent citizenry. Diluting the teaching/learning environments of our schools with faulty assessments, improper placements of students, and biased political agendas is reaping the current results of mediocrity.

Case Study 3

A first-grade teacher in Long Island has twenty-one children in her class. The middle-class community shares the financial burden of diagnosing and placing students with special needs into appropriate settings. The teacher is well respected and has twenty years of experience in the

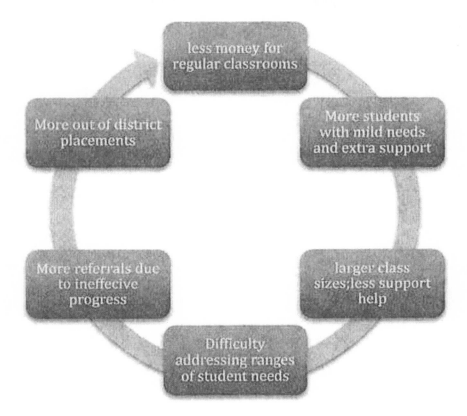

Figure 8.2.

classroom. The principal of the school often asks her to take students who need extra help in literacy and math concepts.

In September, a six-year-old boy diagnosed with ADHD and academic and behavioral issues was placed in her class. His kindergarten and preschool settings were special education classes with a one-on-one aide. The parents requested a transition to a regular class setting with an aide to help with the adjustment. The aide was not hired, leaving the responsibility for his behaviors to the classroom teacher.

Six weeks into the school year, the aide had not been hired, disruption was increasing, attention to the other students had been fragmented, and the teaching/learning process became inconsistent. Support from school administration was lacking, and special education personnel recommended strategies that were not only time consuming but unrealistic for the traditional classroom.

How can we ignore the needs of twenty children in the beginning of their school careers, first grade, to serve one inappropriately placed student? To serve all students, those with special needs and the traditional students, we need to rethink and reflect before succumbing to popular policy propaganda. Below are questions to ask before placement, guidelines that serve as best possibilities for all:

- Can the student achieve academically in a regular classroom with appropriate aids and support?
- Will the student distract the learning of the other students in the classroom?
- What are the benefits of inclusion for the student?
- What is the effect on teaching/learning for all others in the classroom?
- Are we mainstreaming or including students with special needs in regular education settings to control costs?
- How will special placement benefit the student over inclusion?
- Is the least restrictive environment (LRE) predicated on the best environment for student outcomes?
- Are classrooms implementing programs that help regular education students reach their potential?

Answering these questions helps us reflect on what it takes to provide the best education possible for all students, all of whom have special needs, whether classified as learning disabled or not.

Reform should not be founded in the political arenas on the state or national level. Research done by educators should be the voice for the students, and programs based on proven theories should take priority over policy agendas. Milliron (2012) states, "Nothing kills our energized embrace of education reform like top-down, do-it-or-we-die approaches. . . . We have seen these approaches fail. . . . However, we try them again and again. A dominating patriarchal, dominating leadership style is rarely well received" (p. 2).

CONCLUSION

The nation's public schools are facing a dilemma. We are testing more, developing standard programs, adjudicating for inclusion, and achieving less in classrooms and schools. Politicians, policy makers, and special interest groups are interfering and intervening, leaving educators scrambling for solutions. Measured outcomes continue to decline nationally and internationally. Our ranking on the Program for International Student Assessment (PISA) shows a downward trend each passing year.

Advocates for full inclusion in our schools fail to realize the full impact on the teaching/learning experience for all students, even those with special needs. Teachers struggling to pass state- and federal-mandated yearly assessments for all students in their classrooms have had to resort to "teaching to the test." Lieberman (1992) agrees:

> We are testing more, not less. We are locking teachers into constrained curricula and syllabi more, not less. The imprint of statewide account-ability and government spending is increasingly based on tangible, measurable, tabulatable, numerical results. . . . The barrage of curricu-lum materials, grade-level expectations for performance, standardized achievement tests, competency tests continue to overwhelm even the most flexible teachers. (pp. 14, 15)

The current climate of assessment, prescribed programs from business-driven corporations, and negative media attention has detracted from the teaching profession. Schools of education are attracting fewer qualified candidates to the profession, causing a drought of expertise and passion to teach. Colleges and universities need to rethink teacher preparation programs; integrate into content specialties within the institution, and retain development and pedagogy as their strength.

In the midst of obstacles—high costs for special education, inappro-priate placement of students with special needs, and lack of resources or support—is the mandate for yearly achievement through standardized testing. Principals, teachers, schools, and districts are being measured by a yearly "assessment." The drive to show growth on a test has, unfortu-nately, become the mantra of education. Teaching to the test has driven content, expectations, and lower standards for the traditional student in an effort to assure all pass.

Including more students with special needs into the regular classroom and mandating that 90 percent of students take the standardized test has wreaked havoc on the education process in our public schools. The time has come for educators to develop policy, content, and realistic goals for all students in our schools.

Students with special needs can progress academically with individu-alized strategies and support from teachers trained in special education. Traditional students can achieve greater success in classrooms where ex-pectations and content rigor challenge their potentials. Outcomes for both can be standardized with informative and summative assessments: informative to check continual growth and summative to meet the major goal or objective mandate.

Lyon and Vaughn (1994) summarize, "Many successful practices have been researched and identified. Special education professionals and par-ents alike are concerned that regular education teachers have neither the time, nor the expertise to meet their children's needs" (quoted in Thomp-kins & Deloney, 1995, p. 15).

Little has been written about outcomes with more flexible grouping. The concept of tracking, homogeneity, and special classes raises eye-brows or invites a disdain from those who advocate for full inclusion regardless of need. The concept of full inclusion without the appropriate support and resources is a disservice to all students. The reality of individual strengths and weaknesses looms too large to ignore.

What is the real purpose on inclusion? We need to refocus our energy on providing educational practices to meet the needs of all; to motivate and reenergize our educational system. Colleges, universities, schools, educators, and parents must regard the decline in our achievements as a warning. Outcomes need to be elevated for all students; our health as a nation depends on it.

REFERENCES

Antoinette, M. (2002). Examining how the inclusion of disabled students into the general classroom may affect non-disabled classmates. *Fordham Urban Law Journal, 30*(6), 2039–2060.

Association for Persons with Severe Disabilities. (1991). AAPD website. Retrieved from http://www.aapd.com.

Busteed, B. (2012). The school cliff: Student engagement drops with each school year. *The Gallup Blog*. Retrieved from http://thegallupblog.gallup.com/2013/01/the-school-cliff-student-engagement.html.

Canadian Council on Learning (CCL). (2009). http://www.ccl-cca.ca/CCL/Reports/index.html.

Daniel R. R. v. State Board of Edudation. (1989). 874F 2d 1036 (5th Cir.).

Deninger, M. (2008). Disproportionality: A look at special education and race in the commonwealth. Education Research Brief, September 2008. Massachusetts Department of Elementary and Secondary Education.

Hocutt, A. (1996). Effectiveness of special education: Is placement the critical factor? *The Future of Children, 6*(1), 77–102.

Kalbfleisch v. Columbia Community School District. (2009). 920 N. E. 2d (IJJ 5th District).

Lieberman, L. M. (1992). Preserving special education . . . for those who need it. In W. Stainback & S. Stainback (Eds.), *Controversial issues confronting special education: Divergent perspectives,* 157–159 . Boston: Allyn and Bacon.

Milliron, M. D. (2012). *Catalyzing positive change in education: The four pillars.* Cary, NC: SAS. Retrieved from http://www.sas.com/govedu/edu/mark_milliron_white_paper_syn.pdf.

Program for International Student Assessment (PISA) 2003–2009. http://nces.ed.gov/surveys/pisa/.

Robison. J. E. (2013, October 7). What is neurodiversity? My life with Asperger's. *Psychology Today.* Retrieved from http://www.psychologytoday.com/blog/my-life-aspergers/201310/what-is-neurodiversity.

Thompkins, R., & Deloney, P. (1995). *Issues . . . about Change.* Vol. 4. No. 3. *Inclusion: The pros and cons.* Austin, TX: SEDL.

NINE

Effects of Standardized Testing

Janet D. Mulvey

Focusing on yearly achievement tests as the measure for students' learning and growth in schools has become the mantra for assessing students, teachers, administrators, and our schools. The effect on the teaching/learning process is detrimental to all stakeholders in education. This chapter explains the current trend for assessing students with a narrowly focused standardized test, measuring little knowledge and addressing only one type (multiple choice or short answer) of evaluation.

Traditional students and those with special needs are exposed to classroom training instead of instruction for one purpose: to pass a yearly test.

WHAT IS THE TEST FOR?

Prior to No Child Left Behind (NCLB), standardized testing was used to measure the overall achievement of students based on norm-referenced data. The tests helped teachers, schools, and districts to review the curricula content and instructional methodology and to assess where individual students needed extra help.

Minneapolis Special Education Director Ann Casey explains, "Standardized tests are really to make some kind of normative comparison about how our students, in general, are doing compared to other district students. They provide a little information about strengths and gaps but not a lot" (quoted in Brown, 2012). Students with special needs are so diverse in their abilities and weaknesses that administering a single test to evaluate their progress is time consuming, costly, and uninformative.

Time spent preparing for this test, especially in the inclusive class-room, should be a violation of rights for the average student as well. Diverse learning styles, strengths, and weaknesses of the traditional student cannot be accurately measured on this one-time test and does nothing but perpetuate loss of valuable learning for all.

Parents, school leaders, and even some state governors have joined the protest against the yearly be-all, end-all assessments of students across the nation. School districts and states have decided to challenge the mandates for yearly summations of student progress, stating that it, "distorts and corrupts" K–12 classrooms (National Center for Fair and Open Testing, 2012).

New York State Commissioner John B. King Jr. responded to the anger and resentment over testing policies from parents and educator alike. King acknowledged the pressures placed on students subjected to curriculum changes created to meet annual yearly progress on tests. King stated in a letter sent to all superintendents across the state that state education officials "recognize that a variety of pressures at the state and local level may have resulted in more testing than is needed and in rote test preparation that crowds out quality instruction" (quoted in Tyrell, 2013, p. A5).

Seasoned principals and superintendents have been questioning the logic of teaching to the test and strive in selecting research-based information to gain access to informative assessments to drive teaching and learning in their classrooms. Data obtained from research cited by the University of Minnesota and other major institutions are beginning to change the mindset of educators across the country. Lack of engagement and motivation found as students move through the public school system, according the research by the University of Minnesota, is raising an alarm: too many students are dropping out. The study has indicated both parents and teachers struggle to keep their students in school based on the current emphasis of test preparation and less emphasis on engaging curricula and content meaningful for students' futures (Morse, Christenson, and Lehr, 2004).

Jeff Nicols and Anne Stone comment about testing in their son's third-grade classroom:

> Because so much is riding on these tests, the curriculum in our 3rd grader's classroom has been distorted dramatically. There is no music, science, or gym teacher; art has been suspended so there can be extended hours for test prep. Our son's homework has consisted of practice tests — little or no literary merit is based on four possible answers to a question and math worksheets are dreary day after day. (quoted in Clawson, 2012, np)

EFFECTS OF TESTING IN THE INCLUSIVE CLASSROOM

Teachers have been pressured to show annual achievement progress for all students on standardized tests in their classrooms. Research indicates learning rates, strategies, and differences are absolutes in an inclusive classroom. Teachers responsible for the teaching/learning process cannot meet the needs of all students and, thus, have been pressured to "teach to the test" so yearly progress can be reported.

The pressures to pass state and national tests have resulted in schools and districts altering curriculum to parallel test expectations. Popham (2005) explains, "Bad things happen when schools are evaluated using these instructionally insensitive tests. This is particularly true when the importance of a school evaluation is substantial, as it is now" (np).

Case Study

Ms. K is a principal in a middle-class elementary school who has developed a strong collaborative working environment. Teachers, staff, and parents work together, providing a communicative environment benefitting all students. Special education classes collaborate with mainstream combining strategies to challenge all students in reaching their greatest potentials. Earlier ELA, math, and science assessments were used to inform and improve instruction, with all stakeholders contributing to the process.

The onset of full inclusion and tying teacher evaluations to scores on once-a-year tests has destroyed the climate of the school, creating tension, suspicion, and lowering standards simply to pass the tests. Students with special needs are being placed into regular education classrooms without collaborative support. Recently, six students from a special education classroom were mandated for three regular education classrooms. Without collaborative support from a trained special educator, each class has been disrupted with both behaviors and instructional levels.

K's annual evaluation is tied to the results on the yearly tests; all students are required to show annual yearly progress, regardless of their status as regular or special education. Teachers' evaluations are also tied to the results. The media reports scores from throughout the state, published by name and school. All of this places undue burdens on students, teachers, and administrators.

The average and above average student in the inclusive classroom are subjected to lowered standards and constant test preparation to assure positive reports to the community and the state. Content, authentic teaching and imaginative strategies are abandoned, resulting in boredom and frustration for students who come anticipating new knowledge and skills for the twenty-first century but who are instead subjected to meaningless drills to pass a test.

INFORMATIVE ASSESSMENTS

Informative assessments administered throughout the year are used as measures to show both growth and areas in need of reinforcement and make sense when tied to real learning and life experiences. Students can be challenged according to the benchmarks achieved and motivated to explore areas of content more in depth. The average and above students need not wait for attainment by their less able peers, and students with special needs can be remediated by teachers trained to assist them.

Informal surveys taken in rural, suburban, and urban regions validate the use of standardized tests as one measure of student growth at the end of a school year. Standardized tests would then serve as a summative measure to evaluate results based on growth from consistent informative assessments that have been administered to measure progress and need for reteaching through the entire school year. Use and variety of informative assessments are more reliable and valid because they test students in a variety of ways. Authentic, hands-on presentations of materials are not only engaging but also offer students the opportunity to display their knowledge in a variety of ways. Research gathered from Howard Gardner's tireless study of multiple intelligences has pervaded college education programs for decades. Teachers were trained to develop implementation of content through a landscape for diverse learning styles. Whether it is linguistic, logical, musical, spatial, interpersonal, or the like, the theory resonated in schools and produced exciting and engaging programs.

Today, in the current test-taking mode, we have lost the idea of multiple modes of intelligence and learning that have surrendered to a multiple-choice and short-answer assessment as a measure of proficiency. Alfie Kohn (2000) lists "undisputable facts" about the impact of testing on learning":

1. Today's children are tested to a greater extent than any time in our history.
2. Non-instructional factors (e.g., wealth, socioeconomic status, and cultural) explain the variance in comparative test scores between schools and districts.
3. Norm referenced tests are not intended to evaluate either quality of teaching or learning.
4. Standardized test scores measure superficial thinking, not the critical thinking and problem solving associated with higher-level learning.
5. Giving standardized tests to students younger than eight or nine years of age is meaningless and frustrating.
6. Basing graduation or promotion on one single yearly test is condemned by all educational experts.

7. Time and money spent to pass one yearly test takes away from valuable teaching and learning in the classroom.
8. The practice of evaluating teachers, schools and administrators on a standardized test is driving would-be educators from the field, leaving selection for the classroom to the bottom third of candidates. (p. 1)

WHO BENEFITS FROM STANDARDIZED TESTING?

The answer to this question is simple: publishing companies who prepare the tests, the preparation materials, remediation materials, and professional development manuals for teacher development. For-profit corporations have taken over, resulting in huge benefits for the companies and devastation for education.

REFORM AND REVOLT

Change of the current culture of testing as a measure of student achievement is necessary to reignite excitement about learning. The recurring system of a onetime assessment to evaluate students' academic achievement, a teacher's effectiveness in the classroom, or the proficiency of an entire school district should be abandoned and trashed.

The *New York Times* and other newspapers around the state have issued reports by the U.S. Secretary of Education, Arne Duncan, concerning the drop in both English and math scores on standardized tests. The fault lies, Duncan states, with the new rigor placed on the tests' questions. Students, teachers, and parents are frustrated and alarmed at the prospect of lower scores and more "teaching to the test" (Hernández & Gebeloff, 2013). Does the secretary believe making a test more difficult measures knowledge? Doesn't it really mean more test prep on narrowly focused content having no connection to the teaching/learning process?

Many parents across states have taken to the figurative streets. They are protesting against what has become the be-all and end-all of assessing students, schools, and districts. Studies are finding that not only are students becoming increasingly disengaged but now teachers are also following suit. The future human capital for our country is becoming less engaged in the learning process, and the dropout rate is increasing among too many of our able students.

Hernández (2013) writing for the *New York Times*, for example, reported how new, tougher tests have resulted in tears, upset stomachs, and anxiety among high school students across the state. State officials, touting these new assessments, argued to deaf ears just how all these assessments would provide more accurate data to determine readiness for promotion, graduation, or college. In reality, even colleges and universities are disregarding SAT and ACT scores as the sole basis of entry.

Parents who are fed up with the current system of teaching to high-stakes tests—often neglecting the real purpose and joy of education—have organized protests and boycotted the tests. Students generally have become less engaged and motivated about school. Gone are the love and excitement for learning, replaced by the frustration of drills and assessment and the threat of failure. Diane Ravitch, (2013), educational historian and policy analyst, blogs: "The testing mania is spinning out of control. It is turning into child abuse. It demoralizes teachers. It offers the fodder to kill schools. It must be reined in" (np).

DESPERATION CONSEQUENCES

The *New York Times* continues to report on cheating scandals from elementary through high school on high stake tests. New York State has been charged with investigating teachers, administrators, and even school superintendents for misconduct during testing periods.

> Investigators for a school district on Long Island's North Shore are looking into allegations that more than a dozen educators from two elementary schools improperly helped students on standardized tests, including coaching pupils on correct answers last year during state exams, union and district officials said on Thursday. (Baker, 2013, np)

Accusations range from coaching, violating test protocol, supplying "hints," and, in more extreme cases, erasing and changing answers. Because tests have been designated to evaluate the performance of teachers, schools, and districts and tied to funding, cheating has been on the rise.

In the late 1980s, the Department of Education in the late 1980s began reporting that schools in poverty-stricken West Virginia scored above the national average. "The Lake Wobegon" effect, based on Garrison Keillor's stories of a fictitious place where all the children are above average, brought suspicion, resulting in an investigation. Previously assessed as having one of the highest illiteracy rates in the country, the miracle of the high ranking revealed dubious methods of administering and scoring tests.

What kind of a standard are we modeling for our public school students? What are we saying about the value of education? What are our students learning about the rewards for perseverance and hard work? Where is the love of learning to gain new and exciting knowledge?

The public reporting and comparison of scores among schools and states have served as an impetus to receive the highest scores possible, often with devious means. Chicago, New York City, Ohio, Birmingham, Alabama, Texas, and Atlanta, Georgia, are among the cities and states known to have been involved in less-than-honest administration of high-stakes tests.

Scandals continue to surface to the public's attention. Recently a Los Angeles charter school was found to be involved in prepping students with the actual test questions. School administrators in Atlanta, Georgia, erased and changed students' answers, threatening teachers with retaliation if they didn't comply, a scandal that led to the indictment of the former school chief. Washington, D.C., touted as one of the most improved districts under the leadership of Michelle Rhee, has come under attack for dishonesty and unscrupulous test-taking practices.

In schools across too many districts facing reports and possible loss of funding, students who might not perform well on these tests have been encouraged to stay home to avoid poorer scores. Some five hundred students in the Atlanta schools were forced to drop out prior to the date of test administration. The preponderance of evidence concerning cheating is an overwhelming signal that something has to change in our school systems. The desperation caused by the all-important evaluation on one day or one week in schools is so ludicrous it defies understanding by anyone with knowledge of education and assessment.

Cases in Point

The following is an actual scene from a first-grade classroom. It was near the end of February, children ages five and six sat at tables with privacy folders, preparing to take a practice test in readiness for higher-grade mandates. The teacher, experienced and highly qualified, distributed a Scantron scoring sheet and directed the students to solve math problems on a separate sheet and then transfer their answers to the matching bubble on the Scantron. The results: the boys scribbled anything, while some of the girls turned the bubbles into flowers, animals, and figures.

While the humor of their actions matches their ages and innocence, the message is already being inculcated: yearly tests are more important than the curriculum that teaches appreciation of literature, problem solving, and critical thinking. All students, regardless of developmental readiness or ability, will be subjected and labeled according to their score on one yearly bubbled-in test.

ENGLISH AS A SECOND LANGUAGE

In New Jersey, ESL (English as a second language) teachers, have been directed to "test prep" foreign-speaking students throughout the entire year. Students who need to learn English through interactive and applicable curriculum, speaking, reading, and writing, are, instead, being subjected to daily test prep. The teacher, who is bilingual and understands the need to use a multimodality approach, has been told she must prepare the students for the tests, which are given in English. Her evaluation, pay, and perhaps employment are based on how well the students do on the district and state tests. Preparation for the tests, according to this ten-year veteran takes up more than 60 percent of class time. Yes, it is true: one test suits all—average, above, students with special needs, and immigrant children with little or no English.

DATA ON TEST MOTIVATION

Morse, Christenson, and Lehr (2004), conducting research at the University of Minnesota, have found engagement and motivation to learn declining as students move through the school system, decreasing mostly during the transition from middle to high school. Creating purpose, interest, and achieving success are the greatest motivators for high school completion and beyond. Dropout rates and absenteeism decline as engagement increases and successes are achieved. Studies have shown the struggles that teachers and parents have to keep their students in school due to the emphasis of current mandated tests and test prep.

The National Research Council report (2003) on motivation found that upward of 40 percent of high school students are "chronically disengaged." Test-taking policy, ranking students, and teaching to a single yearly standard promotes a feeling of incompetence, boredom, and anxiety. Policy makers who believe that raising standards and increasing test difficulty will produce more proficiency are achieving the exact opposite.

Students have been retained, and schools have been ranked, placed on probation, and often closed, based on so-called nonproficiency, regardless of any environmental or socioeconomic factors. The one-size-fits-all approach ignores who and what we are as a country—culturally, economically, and ethnically. How do we judge all students and schools on common criteria with so little commonality in every other factor (e.g., children's backgrounds, family income, races, languages, genders), not to mention school goals, types, and levels?

The emphasis on yearly assessments—which occur near the end of the school year to determine "success," regardless of readiness, when it's almost too late to help students further in a subject—has been a disaster for whole communities. And the results of standardized testing keep us less than competitive on international educational tests. The data are clear. Yearly, one-day assessments that judge, instead of inform, academic performances are ludicrous. The pressure to show proficiency or else has produced little besides school, teacher, and student focus toward a goal that has little to do with teaching and learning.

TRAINING REPLACING LEARNING

Beginning to train pupils to fill in bubbles on a Scantron sheet in first grade is just one example of time spent working toward a meaningless goal. Test prep continues through all grades, providing less time to develop skills necessary for postsecondary schooling or career training. It is also much weaker at holding students' interests and excitement that traditional, real learning.

Recent studies have lamented the lack of preparation of American students for postsecondary education. Internationally, the United States continues to lag behind other modem nations in literacy, math, and the sciences. Districts, fearful of losing funding and even being shut down, have taken to unfortunate acts of cheating, just to stay alive. Does one really believe that by making tests more "rigorous"—and then continuing teacher, school, and district rankings based on a single narrow focus—will actually improve learning for all children?

WHAT CAN, AND SHOULD, BE DONE NOW

Proven, time-tested strategies to improve and enhance motivation should become the mantra for all schools:

- Implement developmentally appropriate tasks to build success and a feeling of competence and confidence.
- Allow students to discover how their actions and strategies result in positive outcomes.
- Give them control on undertaking a task that has value to them, promoting success though experimentation.
- Reward success to promote social acceptance and approval.
- Acknowledge the importance of real assessments.

Are we worshipping a false god? With no real argument about the importance of assessments in the modem world, appropriate testing should be ongoing throughout the school year to measure progress and help teachers and students plan for improvement:

- **Tell everyone how their children are doing.** Schools, teachers, students, and parents need to be told how well their charges (kids) are doing in schools, academically, psychologically, socially. No doubt, testing isn't going away. Rather, it's what to evaluate and when to have the evaluations—and how *to use* the results. Assessments that matter should, thus, be geared to provide information on students' needs and/or accomplishment toward a common goal.
- **Make school authentic, based on class content and curricula.** Ongoing, in all forms, tests should often be project based, and authentic. The testing process should thus be administered to inform edu-

cators of progress and/or the needs for reteaching. Inquiry, exploration, review, and discovery should be on the daily menu in every classroom and for every content area.

- **Put content at the center of the classroom and testing.** Content in the classroom is learned through process, application, demonstration, and continuous modification for better growth and more in-depth understanding. Environments in schools should promote challenge, excitement, and curiosity. Content assessment should be conducted in the same manner as we work to relate multiple intelligences to different learning (and testing) styles.

- **Diversify testing for subjects and students.** Alternative means of assessment to meet national standards can consist of portfolios, standard-based projects, authentic application, written diaries, rubrics, and ongoing informal tests and quizzes to measure mastery at each stage of learning. Once we have determined desired outcomes for each content area, continuous anecdotal records of progress will help each student reach the desired goal through ongoing monitoring. Thus, this genuine preparation and testing would increase the successful completion of schooling and performance on the standardized tests.

- **Provide classroom teachers with resources to meet needs of all students**. Recognize the vast differences in needs for traditional and special needs students. Stop expecting the general education teacher to engage, remediate, and challenge all students while adapting specific strategies to meet complex issues of students with special needs.

- **Act now.** Time is fleeting, and schools need to know how they are doing to allow teachers to improve instruction for all and to alert students and families about what's coming and where they are going. Otherwise, we will continue to see families refusing to send their children to school on days when these major state tests are being given. Further support for the public school system will decline. Confusion will likely change to mayhem as the United States continues to decline in its education "outputs."

SUMMARY

Parents are becoming more aware of the negative consequences of high-stakes tests. They hear the complaints from their children, see the lack of enthusiasm for learning, and have experienced the cut in extra-curricular programs in lieu of more time for classes based on testing standards, and they are reacting. Still, educational policy makers haven't gotten the message.

When possible, many parents are selecting private or charter schools where educational benefits are based on programs enriched with authentic learning and assessing, problem solving, and critical thinking to promote self-efficacy and extracurricular activities to spike the interests in the arts. The loss for public school talent is immense; average to gifted are leaving to receive a more rounded and valid education. Teachers are leaving the profession, and those entering are too often the bottom third of college candidates.

The use of a single standard-based instrument one day or week during the school to assess progress has no basis in accuracy or validity. Students should be assessed throughout the year to inform teachers of areas both strong and weak. Assessing content through a multimodality approach is not only reasonable, it is research based.

Instead, we have developed a system based on fear, anxiety, and disengagement. We must revolt against a system that has proven ineffectual and implement research-based strategies to improve teaching and learning. To become competitive in the international marketplace, it is imperative to rethink our curriculum, make it relevant to school, community, state, and national interests.

The public school, rich in history from Horace Mann to John Dewey and Albert Bandura, needs re-ignition and focus on educational knowledge and growth for the twenty-first century. Engagement of students, motivation to think proactively and productively, and assessing for improvement are the tools for the success for our schools and, thus, our society.

REFERENCES

Baker, A. (2013, April 11). Allegations of test help by teachers. *New York Times*. Retrieved from http://www.nytimes.com/2013/04/12/education/long-island-educators-under-inquiry-for-test-help.html.

Brown, A. (2012, December 9). When tests tell teacher nothing: Special needs not met by standardized testing. *Twin Cities Daily Planet*. Retrieved from http://www.tcdailyplanet.net/news/2012/12/09/when-tests-tell-teachers-nothing-special-needs-not-met-standardized-tests.

Clawson, L. (2012, April 29). Test-driven education means giant corporate profits and "pineapples don't have sleeves." *Daily Kos*. Retrieved from http://www.dailykos.com/story/2012/04/29/1085807/-Testing-driven-education-means-giant-corporate-profits-and-pineapples-don-t-have-sleeves.

Gardner, H. (1983, 2004, 2011). *Frames of mind: The theory of multiple intelligences*. New York: Basic Books. pp. 77–251.

Kohn, A. (2000). Standardized Testing and its Victims. In: *Education Week*, September 7.

Hernández, J. (2013, April 19). A Tough new test spurs protest and tears. *New York Times*. Education Section A24

Hernández, J., & Gebeloff, R. (2013, August 7). Test scores sink as New York adopts tougher benchmarks. *New York Times*. Retrieved from http://www.nytimes.com/

2013/08/08/nyregion/under-new-standards-students-see-sharp-decline-in-test-scores.html?_r=0.

Morse, A. B., Christenson, S. L., & Lehr, C. A. (2004). *School completion and student engagement: Information and strategies.* University of Minnesota. Retrieved from http://www.nasponline.org/resources/principals/nasp_complparents.pdf.

National Center for Fair & Open Testing. (2012). http://www.fairtest.org/-12?page=7.

National Research Council. (2003). *Engaging Schools: Fostering High School Students' Motivation to Learn.* Washington, DC: The National Academies Press.

Popham, W. J. (2005, March 23). Standardized testing fails the exam. *Edutopia.* Retrieved from http://www.edutopia.org/standardized-testing-evaluation-reform.

Ravitch, D. (2013). Children: Get high scores or your teacher will get fired. *Diane Ravitch's Blog.* Retrieved from http://dianeravitch.net/2013/04/23/children-get-high-scores-or-your-teacher-will-be-fired/.

Tyrell, J. (2013, October 25). Education chief acknowledged "more testing than is needed." *Long Island Newsday.* Retrieved from http://www.newsday.com/long-island/education/education-chief-acknowledged-more-testing-than-is-needed-1.6322050.

TEN

Urban Problems and Solutions: Funding For All

Bruce S. Cooper

Containing costs and using funds more effectively for all students are the twin problems discussed in this chapter. We know that the classification and support of more children with special needs and disabilities have dramatically raised the cost of education. With about 13 percent of students nationwide now classified as needing special attention and education, the costs for serving these students has reached 24 percent of the yearly budgets in some districts, while the number and spending on regular and gifted education for the rest of the children have actually declined in many districts and schools.

As Huff-Education recently reported:

> In Cleveland, the district has lost 41 percent of its students since 1996 while its proportion of students with special needs rose from 13.4 percent to 22.9 percent last year. In Milwaukee, enrollment has dropped by nearly 19 percent over the past decade, but the percentage of students with disabilities has risen from 15.8 percent in 2002 to 19.7 percent in 2012. (Hoag, 2012)

So while expenses in education have risen, the numbers of regular and above average children have actually declined. This chapter analyzes trends in financial support and suggests what can be done to help all students better, more economically, and more effectively in the future. How can we serve the special needs child without neglecting the special academic and talented youngster in our public schools? And what are the best definitions of children with "special needs" and "disabilities," a complex question (see Forness & Knitzer, 1992).

BACKGROUND

American education has broadened its world outlook, seeking to give more students with different backgrounds, needs, and locations greater access, better resources, and more opportunities to learn. And the financing of schools has followed suit, as funds are made available under policies and several "equity" lawsuits in an attempt to end segregation, separation, and limitations for these groups. This chapter reviews the funding patterns as they reflect the policies and programs of local, state, and federal government—and as they have attempted, often, to extend a quality education to all children.

Integration by Race

The process started in the 1950s when education in the South and many northern cities was totally or partially segregated by race. The "separate but equal" concept was overturned in 1954 and 1955 by the *Brown v. Board of Education* cases, which began to remove the walls of racial segregation and to offer black children greater educational opportunities. While this Supreme Court decision did not have immediate financial effects, it did give black children a better chance of getting a high-quality, better-financed education, alongside their white comrades.

Equalization of School Funding

Later, in 1965, a similar equity legal principle was applied in California when the family of John Serrano Jr. sued the state of California (using a California official, Mary Baker Priest, former U.S. Treasurer) and their local school system as poor neighborhoods and communities had fewer resources to spend on their schools. In *Serrano v. Priest* (1971; 1976), the California high court ruled that denying children an equal education based on differences in local property "values," and, thus, tax funding levels, was not constitutional under the California legal framework.

The *Serrano* decision was later challenged in a similar case in Texas, in *San Antonio Independent School District v. Rodriguez* (1973), where the local parents in a poor neighborhood sued the state, arguing that the "Texas method of school financing violated the equal protection clause of the Fourteenth Amendment to the U.S. Constitution" (p. 111).

In a Texas state appeal, the U.S. Supreme Court ruled that the U.S. Constitution did not guarantee all children an equal education, and that the diversity of local funds was legal. The majority opinion, reversing the Texas District Court, stated that the lawyers for the school districts had not sufficiently proven the following: (1) that education is a fundamental right, (2) that the equity principle textually existed within the U.S. Constitution, and (3) that the argument thereby (through the Fourteenth

Amendment to the Constitution) could be applied to the several states. The court also found the financing system was *not* subject to strict scrutiny.

However, within twenty-five years, over thirty-one of the fifty states had witnessed *Serrano* types of law cases, and many of the cases, under their state constitutions, were decided that children could not be denied an equal education based on local property wealth and the ability of the district to pay for a quality education. While the lawyers usually avoided using the U.S. Constitutional arguments, most states applied the equity of their own state laws and constitutions—and were often able to get more equal funding for more impoverished local school districts from state aid.

Greater Opportunity for Disabled Children

Next, the school districts, as well as state and federal governments, recognized the relatively greater costs of education for children with special needs, problems, and shortcoming. Rather than go to court, the education interests groups went to the U.S. Congress and lobbied for the passage of Public Law 94–142, the Education of All Handicapped Children Act, now called the Individuals with Disabilities Education Act (IDEA). The four purposes of the Public Law 94–142 (1975) are as follows:

- To assure that all children with disabilities have available to them . . . a free appropriate public education which emphasizes special education and related services designed to meet their unique needs;
- To assure that the rights of children with disabilities and their parents . . . are protected;
- To assist States and localities to provide for the education of all children with disabilities; and
- To assess and assure the effectiveness of efforts to educate all children with disabilities. (pp. 44–45)

Since the law was passed in the 1970s, states and local systems of education have also worked to identify, review, and ensure that all children with disabilities were given extra help. As the number of children recognized as needing extra help has risen to almost 14 percent, the costs of educating and caring for these children has risen also, to nearly 23 percent of school spending.

More Efficient Use of School District Funds

In the 1980s, Sheree Speakman and Bruce Cooper, working for the Coopers & Lybrand accounting firm, created the Finance Analysis Model (FAM) that for the first time allowed district leaders to track funds to the classroom, particularly those resources used for direct instruction. With the help of Mayor Rudolph Giuliani and an assistant, Herman Badillo, we determined that only about half the dollars even reached the school, and less than a third of the funds were spent on *direct instruction* in the classroom, while most funds were expended on administration in the bureaucracy and building security and upkeep.

When the process was repeated after FAM was established and the levels of district and city school bureaucracies were reduced in New York City public schools, the funding for direct instruction had risen to 61 percent in the classroom, with nearly 80 percent then reaching the school. The model was patented as IN$ITE™, and is now used across the country, with Rhode Island and South Carolina, for example, implementing the model statewide, tracking funds to every district and school in these states. The model allows leaders at the state and local level to analyze how much of the funding is used for central and school level administration, building maintenance, bus service, and so forth. As the model explains:

> An advanced software package for cost accounting and analysis, management reporting, performance assessment and decision support tool is described. The IN$ITE™ software package collects, organizes, manages and consolidates financial data and permits the standardized evaluation and comparison of different educational institutions. The software package implements the Finance Analysis Model For Education as a relational database for the efficient and cost-effective management of educational institutions.
>
> Financial data are organized into three dimensions: Functions, Programs and Locations. IN$ITE has five Functions that are subdivided into 15 Sub-functions and further devolved to 32 Detail Functions, each of which provides greater clarity of fund use. The Program Dimension

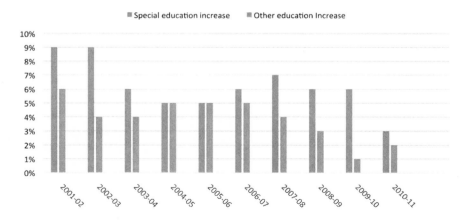

Figure 10.1.   Education Cost Increases: Special Ed versus Other Education Increases over ten years. (National Center Education Statistics, 2011)

of IN$ITE permits the identification and determination of the costs of various special programs within the school system and in each school. Thus, the Organizational (or Locational) Dimension of IN$ITE comprises three levels: Expenses that are to be charged to the central location, to various school-sites, or to be retained as non-allocated expenses. IN$ITE also permits reporting of decisionsupport data by school-site or cost-center.

This functional level of analysis ensures that the money will and can reach the child in the classroom for direct instruction. Thus, if we are to ensure that all children get educated, effectively, then funding must be available to them for direct instruction and support.

Funding for Children with Special Needs

William Ouchi, Carolyn Brown, and Bruce Cooper (2004) were interested in determining how much funding children with disabilities received compared to "regular education" students in K–12 schools. This process, called *weighted student funding* or *formula* (WSF), is timely, as the number of children classified and the costs of educating a highly disabled child can be high, including custodial costs (e.g., transporting a child to school in a van who cannot walk or is in a wheel chair), and those who need constant personal attention at school, during school, and are assigned a teaching assistant, or a speech pathologist to help them.

If a regular education child costs, say, $12,000 per year, while a special education student requires $18,000-worth of help, then the regular child is a 1.0, and the special education child, in this case, is 1.5. We found that some kids "cost" $36,000 per year and, thus, were weighted a 3.0 if they

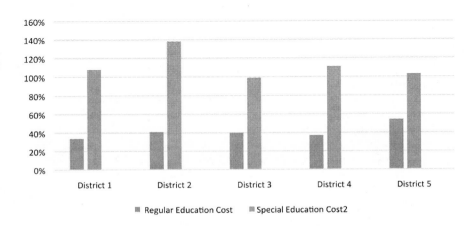

Figure 10.2. Comparison of Education Costs

required special transportation, help in class, and support during the day. (See figure 10.2.)

Likewise, should a child need placement in special school, the cost can exceed $60,000 per year, and the weighting might be 5.0 or five times the average cost for regular education student.

MOVING TOWARD ONE EDUCATION FOR ALL

The world is concerned about education for all, and to make education truly universal and affordable, these five As are considered important for each nation:

- *Availability*—Funded by governments, education is universal, *free*, and compulsory (Beiter, 2005). Proper infrastructure and facilities should be in place with adequate books and materials for students. Buildings should meet both safety and sanitation standards, such as having clean drinking water. Active recruitment, proper training, and appropriate retention methods should ensure that enough qualified teachers and other staff are available at each school.
- *Accessibility*—All children should have equal access to school services regardless of gender, race, religion, ethnicity, or socioeconomic status. Efforts should be made to ensure the inclusion of marginalized groups, including children of refugees, the homeless, or those with disabilities. No forms of segregation or denial of access should affect any students, thus, ensuring that proper laws are in place to prevent child labor or exploitation—and, thus, ensuring that all children receive quality primary through secondary education. Schools must be within a reasonable distance for children within the community; otherwise, transportation should be provided to students, particularly those who live in rural areas, to guarantee routes to school are both safe and convenient. Thus, education should be affordable to all, with textbooks, supplies, and uniforms provided to students at no additional costs.
- *Acceptability*—The quality of education provided should be free of discrimination, thus, becoming relevant and culturally appropriate for all students. Students should not be expected to conform to any specific religious or ideological views. Methods of teaching should be objective and unbiased and material available should reflect a wide array of ideas and beliefs. Health and safety should be emphasized within schools including the elimination of any forms of corporal punishment. Professionalism of staff and teachers should be maintained.
- *Adaptability*—Educational programs should be flexible and able to adjust according to societal changes and the needs of the community. Schools should respect observance of religious or cultural holi-

days to accommodate students, along with providing adequate care to those students with disabilities.

- *Affordability*—And finally, how can communities afford to educate all children, including the most and least able, the regular and special education child, and those with normal physical abilities, and those who are physically handicapped?

PURPOSES OF THIS CHAPTER

This main question is how can a society equalize and distribute funds fairly and make real opportunities available that are: (a) improving education for special needs children while (b) ensuring the quality and effectiveness of the teaching and learning of regular and above average in school? That is, how can schools in the United States contain *costs* while meeting the goal of educating all? In many districts and states we see the average and above average being short-changed due to legal stipulations that drive up costs for the special education child.

This chapter examines and analyzes the costs by group—gifted, average, and below average—particularly when the students are educated in a common classroom with extra support intellectually, emotionally, and physically. How are the costs of educating one group affected by the other groups as inclusion becomes more common and classification becomes more costly?

The steps in this process are as follows: (1) Understand how much special education *costs*, using three different models: inclusion, separation for special programs during a regular day, and full separation. (2) Analyze the costs and effectiveness of each level of separation and inclusion. (3) Recommend new models that may save funding and improve education for all students, regardless of their needs and abilities.

MORE COSTS *FOR* SPECIAL EDUCATION, LESS FOR THE REST?

We know that special education students can cost more than other children in school. Just how much more depends on the child's needs and the expenses of programs designed for that child. Data show great differences, as the numbers of students classified—and identified needing extra help—have grown exponentially since the passage and implementation of PL 94–142 in 1974.

As Christina A. Samuels (2011) explains:

> The Federal IDEA provides a set of protections for 6.6 million students—about 13 percent of the total student population—who have dyslexia, autism, intellectual disabilities, blindness, or other impairments that affect educational performance. These students are entitled

to a "free, appropriate public education" in the least-restrictive environment that meets their needs. Failure to provide such services often causes parents to sue in federal court. (p. 1)

We shall examine the growth of the number and percent of special students related in size to the other students, the costs and percentage being allocated for these students, and how these costs might be contained while serving all kids better. When the federal law was passed in 1970, the federal government promised a 40 percent reimbursement to states and local districts to assist them in providing the extra, costly services, without compromising programs for the regular and above average student.

Ben Barnes, the Connecticut governor's budget director, states: "I'm afraid special education costs are growing at the expense of regular education. If we do not figure a way to control special education costs, then anything we do for [overall education funding] is irrelevant" (quoted in Thomas, 2012, np). Figure 10.1 shows the increase in costs of both special education and other education services between 2001–2002 and 2010–2011 in Connecticut. Costs grew by 9 percent during this period for regular and "other education," while special education costs have increased

In particular, in Connecticut, the cost of educating the average students is $14,400, while the special education cost has reached well over $50,000 per student. Thus, in particular, we see only a 1 percent increase for regular education in one year, while special education grew by 6 percent. At the extreme, Barnes reports that the most costly, "about 300 students who require one-on-one tutoring, special learning equipment or out-ofdistrict tuition[,] cost approximately $150,000 per pupil each year." In fact the Connectucut state budget director reported that it would cost the state an additional $1.1 million to pay for special education and transportation for 2013–2014 school year (quoted in Thomas, 2012, np).

In forty-four states, school districts are required to prove that special education students in their district are receiving the appropriate placement. Parents often sue the school district, attempting to prove that their children's placements are not appropriate or adequate. When such a suit is filed, the district must pay all the legal fees, regardless of the outcomes. In many of these forty-four states, districts cite "the burden of proof issue as the single most expensive costs of providing special education" (Thomas, 2012). When in doubt, sue.

Recently, we learned that 68 percent of districts report that "shifting the burden in these cases that came before the hearing officer would save them an average of $74,000 per case, per year" (Thomas, 2012). In Solana Beach, California, we are told the following: "The school board just approve expending $354,000 to Care-A-Van . . . to transport about 30 special education students in 2012–13. That's almost $12,000 per student, more than it costs to educate a students for an entire year" (Sutton, 2012).

Sound difficult? It is. Would schools in the United States be better off distributing special education students to regular classrooms, along with providing these students with extra help? Would this reduce overall costs, thus, stopping the erosion of resources for the average and gifted students, instead of overspending to mainly attempt to bring all students up to some minimal standard?

We need a system that benefits all students, regardless of their background, language, disabilities, or talents. Contrasting, we now we see funds draining away from the more able to work mainly with the more disabled, to the benefit of no students. As one source reports, both the number and the costs of educating children with disabilities have risen, with the federal government paying less and less:

> Regardless of federal and state special education funding, however, local communities under IDEA must provide a free appropriate public education in the least restrictive environment to children with disabilities, no matter how high or low those costs are in the case of an individual child or how high they are for a group of children with disabilities. As a result, special education spending by local districts has consumed a large portion of increased education funding nationally—40 *percent of the increase by one estimate*—since the late 1960s. (Heasley, 2013)

Thus,

> [the] number of students served under IDEA has grown at nearly twice the rate of the general education population. During the twenty-five-year period between 1980 and 2005, the IDEA population increased by 37 percent, while the general education population grew by only 20 percent. Moreover, students served under IDEA today account for about 14 percent of the total education population, up from about 10 percent in the 1980s. (Heasley, 2013)

Why this growth in numbers, costs, and percentages? Four reasons merge: (1) the better ability to identify children with needs and problems from birth to age eighteen when they can leave K–12 schools; (2) the widening of the definition of "disabled" under law (IDEA, 1997); (3) the inclusion of three- to nine-year-olds who are determined to be "developmentally delayed"; and (4) the growing awareness and actions of parents who want their children to be served more fully in school and are willing to act and even sue to get this help starting earlier.

Thus, students are being identified earlier, more fully, and with more family involvement and knowledge, bolstered by what they are hearing and learning from other families with similar children. And the U.S. Congress "widened the definition of 'disabled under IDEA in 1997" (Hoag, 2012), thus, extending the school's responsibility for younger children, to

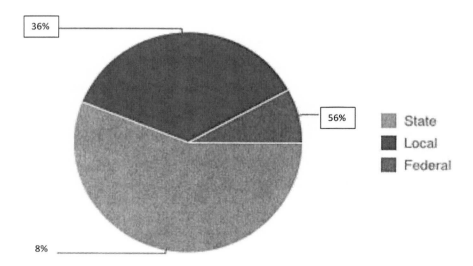

Figure 10.3. *Source: Federal Education Budget Project, 2013.*

ages three to five, whereas in the past most of these children didn't enter school at all until they were six, seven, or older.

Also, we need to examine who's paying for these newly and larger numbers of special needs children? We see in figure 10.2 that in 1987–1988, the states paid the most, at 56 percent; federal government, 36 percent; and local districts picked up the rest with 9 percent. However, in just another ten years, the local districts were picking up the plurality of the costs, with states and federal levels going down a little.

Then, in just twelve year, the locals were carrying the most of the costs, again affecting the funding of students in regular classes, not to mention the gifted and exceptional kids. See figure 10.3, showing that the local costs amounted to 46 percent, while the state had dropped to 45 percent from 46 percent and the federal level remained low at 8 percent in 2000, having been just 9 percent earlier. Thus, we can conclude that local school districts

> have had trouble covering such a high percentage of the $50 billion spent on special education services. Heavily impacted districts with a disproportionate number of high-need, high-cost disabled students struggle the most, particularly if the district is small or rural. Of all disabled students, approximately one-half of one percent, or around 330,000 students, require more than $100,000 in special education services. (Federal Education Budget Project, 2013)

A recent study by Nathan Levenson and associates compared costs in ten school districts in five states and found that increasing spending on special needs students did not always mean they did better and performed higher.

As a *Huffpost Education* article about the report describes:

> Levenson's team reduced the sample into 10 pairs of comparable districts in five states—Florida, Massachusetts, Minnesota, Ohio and Texas. In each pair, one district spent less on special education but boasted higher achievement levels, as measured by scores on the 2011 National Assessment of Educational Progress (NAEP). On average, the higher-achieving districts within the pairs placed 25 percent more special education pupils at the proficient level, while their lower-achieving counterparts spent 22 percent more on special education, when adjusted for total student enrollment. ("Special Education Spending," 2012, np)

And even children who are incarcerated for breaking the law are now given special education services, if needed, and again increase the number and cost of serving all children under the IDEA. Many are born to mothers who are in prison and may require help and must receive educational services under IDEA passed in 1997 (see Special Education in Correctional Institutions, 2000).

Levenson's (2005) makes concrete suggestions for controlling and even reducing the costs of special education, As Frederick Hess writes in the foreword of Levenson's report, "There must be a more promising path." Hess also sketches ways for districts to do far better in four key areas. He explains how to squeeze costs and boost results by:

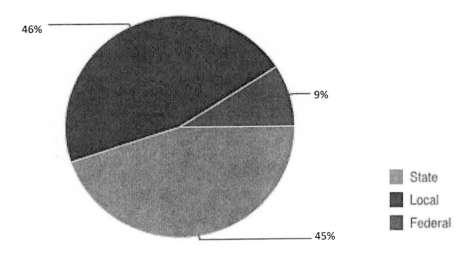

Figure 10.4. *Source: Federal Education Budget Project, 2013.*

- better integrating special education with general education class-rooms;
- smarter deployment of support staff;
- the use of more sophisticated metrics to gauge effectiveness met-rics; and
- employing more strategic management structures. (Hess, 2005, p. iii)

Hess goes on to say that "such strategies . . . equip teachers and adminis-trators to better meet student needs while also helping policymakers pro-vide much-needed targeted support for cost-effective practices" (2005, p. iii).

As Levenson (2005) notes, "Districts must tackle the twin challenges of controlling special education costs and improving student achieve-ment. In short, we are asking districts to do more with less" (p. 1).

Also, as we extend services to younger children, the costs of serving special pupils are rising. For example, New York City is paying private contractors more than $1 billion this year to operate a little-known special education program for three- and four-year-olds, nearly double the amount it paid six years ago (Halbfinger, 2012). In particular, Halbfinger found that

> the program serves 25,000 children with physical, learning, develop-mental and other disabilities. While the number of children in the pro-gram has risen slowly in recent years, annual costs have soared to about $40,000 per child. according to an analysis of city education spending by the *New York Times.* (np)

Thus, the financial effects of the rising number of special education stu-dents, and the increased costs in educating them, raises the following five issues that this book addresses.

1. More Demands, Less New Funding

A key problem is the rising demands for services without concomitant federal and state spending increases. As Brady (2011) describes:

> Schools must meet certain standards for educating special needs stu-dents under the federal Individual with Disabilities Education Act (IDEA). The problem, however, is that federal funding to meet these requirements is nowhere near the levels school districts need, so the state and, ultimately, taxpayers bear the burden of these costs. (np)

The analysis in the article then analyzes the costs per pupil for regular education versus special education, showing how much more costly the latter is now across the state. This analysis demonstrates the rising num-ber and costs of these services when compared to the education of other regular education children We see that special education students cost nearly double per pupil what other children's expenditures run.

2. Less Attention to Gifted and Talented Students

This book also seeks to show that the country may spending more money on a rising number of children with disabilities and fewer resources and less attention to the children who are special in other ways: the brightest, the talented, and the outstanding students in our school systems.

3. More Variation in Spending on Special Education than Regular Education in Richer Districts

Levenson found that "spending and staffing for special education varies considerably more than it does for regular education, and this wide variation primarily stems from differences in staffing levels among districts, even when total enrollments are held constant" (p. 41).

Most of this spending is on teachers and other staff, amounting to about 95 percent of the costs. In fact, "Levenson calculated that districts with above average special education staffing would save over $10 billion a year collectively if they were to reduce their staff to keep with the national norm" ("Special Education Spending," 2012, np). An interesting conclusion is that IDEA, in its own way, prevents districts from making the best and most efficient decisions, a tenet of other education decision - making. He recommends that policies be changed to "permit greater flexibility in the use of Individuals with Disabilities Education Act (IDEA) funds" ("Special Education Spending," 2012, np).

4. Cutting Funds for the Gifted

Next we must recognize that districts are sometimes reducing resources for the gifted, understanding that these students will easily pass state tests, to concentrate on the less able students. One *New York Times* article (Schemo, 2004) on rural Arkansas reported the following:

> Mountain Grove, a remote rural community in the Ozarks where nearly three in four students live in poverty, eliminated all of its programs for the district's 50 or so gifted children like Audrey, who is 8 now. Struggling with shrinking revenues and new federal mandates that focus on improving the test scores of the lowest-achieving pupils, Mountain Grove and many other school districts across the country have turned to cutting programs for their most promising students. (np)

5. *Aiming for Mediocrity*

One conclusion drawn from these reductions in talented and gifted programs is that the U.S. is now shooting for mediocrity in its schools. Taking the Mountain Grove district in Arkansas again as an example:

> "Rural districts like us, we've been literally bleeding to death," said Gary Tyrrell, assistant superintendent of the Mountain Grove School District, which has 1,550 students. The formula for cutting back in hard times was straightforward. If painful, Mr. Tyrrell said: Satisfy federal and state requirements first. Then, "Do as much as we can for the majority and work on down." Under that kind of a formula, programs for gifted and talented children have become especially vulnerable. (Schemo, 2004, np)

Thus, we can conclude that federal, state, and local policies fail in several important ways to serve the average and above average students very well:

1. No Child Left Behind is silent on the education of gifted children. Under the law, schools must test students annually in reading and math from third grade to eighth grade, and once in high school.
2. Schools receiving federal antipoverty money must show that more students each year are passing standardized tests or face expensive and progressively more severe consequences.
3. As long as students pass the exams, the federal law offers no rewards for raising the scores of high achievers, or punishment if their progress lags. In a personal interview, Bridget Williams, the principal of Mountain Grove Middle School, states that "very bright children do not deserve specially tailored classes, especially when the district is focusing on bringing all children up to a minimum standard of competence."

Thus, not only is spending moving away from the education of the gifted in most public schools, but few policies are there to protect the above average student. We are perhaps the only nation in the world that is more concerned about bringing up the slowest kids at the cost of helping the brightest and most gifted. Joseph S. Renzulli, director of the National Research Center on the Gifted and Talented at the University of Connecticut, concurs: "Many of the gifted and talented will never, ever achieve their potential without some type of advanced learning opportunities and resources" (1998). Deborah L. Ruf, author of *Losing our Minds: Gifted Children Left Behind* (2005), agrees: "Equity goes both ways. It means we're going to accommodate the needs of students, whether they're struggling, average or aboveaverage learners" (p. 165).

REFERENCES

Beiter, K. D. (2005). *The protection of the right to education tv international law.* Rotterdam, Holland: Martlnus Nijhoff Publishers. 21–22.

Brady. J. (2011). Special education funding for schools a delicate balancing act. *White Plains* Patch. Retrieved from http://whiteplains.patch.com/groups/schools/p/special-education-funding-for-schools-a-delicate-balancing-act.

Brown v. Board of Education. (1954). 347 U.S. 483, 490.

Cooper, B. S., & Speakman, S. (1995). *Optimizing educational resources.* New York: JAI.

Federal Education Budget Project. (2013). *Background and analysis.* Retrieved from http://febp.newamerica.net/background-analysis/individuals-disabilities-education-act-cost-impact-local-school-districts.

Forness, S. R., & Knitzer, J. (1992). A new proposed definition and terminology to replace "serious emotional disturbance" in Individuals with Disabilities Education Act. *School Psychology Review, 21*(1), 12–20.

Halbfinger, D. M. (2012, June 5). Cost of prekindergarten special education is soaring. *New York Times, Education.* Retrieved from http://www.nytimes.com/2012/06/06/education/prekindergarten-costs-in-new-york-city-have-doubled-in-6-years.html?pagewanted=all&_r=0.

Heasley, S. (2013, Sept. 16). Special education spending declines. *Disability Scoop.* http://www.disabilityscoop.com/2013/09/16/sped-spending-declines/18717/.

Hess, F. (2005). Foreword. In N. Levenson, *Something has got to change: Rethinking special education* (p. iii). Washington, DC: Future of American Education of American Enterprise Institute.

Hoag, C. (2012). Students with special needs staying in traditional public schools. In: Huff Post Education, http://www.huffingtonpost.com/2012/08/20/special-needs-kids-stayin_0_n_1803753.html.

Levenson, N. (2005). *Something has got to change: Rethinking special education.* Washington, DC: Future of American Education of American Enterprise Institute.

National Center Education Statistics. (2011). Education Cost Increases: Special Ed versus Other Education Increases over ten years. *Digest of Education Statistics,* 2011. https://nces.ed/gov/pubs/2012/2012001.pdf.

Ouchi, W., Cooper, B. S., & Brown, C. (2004). From courtroom to classroom: Operationalizing "adequacy" in funding teaching and learning. *Educational Considerations, 32*(1), Fall 2004.

Renzulli, J. S. (1998). The three ring conception of giftedness. In: Baum, S. M., Reis, S. M., & Maxfield, L. R. (Eds), *Nurturing the gifts and talents of primary grade students,* pp. 54–62. Mansfield Center, CT: Creative Learning Press.

Ruf, D. L. (2005). *Losing our minds: Gifted children left behind.* New York: Great Potential Press.

Samuels, C. A. (2011). Special education court decisions on the rise. *Education Week.* http://www.edweek.org/edweek/specialed/2011/01.

Schemo, D. J. (2004). Schools, facing tight budgets, leave gifted programs behind. *New York Times, Archives.* Retrieved from http://www.nytimes.com/2004/03/02/us/schools-facing-tight-budgets-leave-gifted-programs-behind.html.

San Antonio Independent School District v. Rodriguez. (1973). 411 U.S. 1.

Serrano v. Priest. (1971). 5 Cal.3d 584.

Serrano v. Priest. (1976). 18 Cal.3d 728.

Special education in correctional institutions. (2000). National Center on Education, Disability, and Juvenile Justice. http://www.edjj.org/Publications/pub05_01_00.html.

Special education spending reduction to national median could save districts $10 billion: Study. (2012). *Huffpost Education.* Retrieved from http://www.huffingtonpost.com/2012/09/05/districts-could-save-10-b_n_1858345.html.

Sutton, M. (2012, August 30). The cost of special education. *Del Mar Times.* Retrieved from http://www.delmartimes.net/2012/08/30/the-cost-of-special-education/.

Thomas, J. R. (2012, September 17). Panel looks to tackle skyrocketing special educa-
    tion. *CT Mirror*. Retrieved from http://ctmirror.org/panel-looks-tackle-skyrocketing-
    special-education-costs/.
Villa, R. A., & Thousand, J. S. (2003). Making inclusive education work. *Educational
    Leadership, 61*(2), 19–21.

ELEVEN

Recommendations from the Authors

Implementing new goals for new standards: Educating All

All students need protection under the Elementary and Secondary Education Act. Passed in 1965, the ESEA emphasized the need for an equal education for all students. While focusing on students living in poverty, it calls for equitable funding and resources, along with accountability, to assure equal opportunity. Reauthorized as the No Child Left Behind (NCLB) Act, it has evolved into an accountability program with few learning goals.

Our international standing continues to decline under the current system, and we must begin to reorganize, depoliticize, and restructure our entire system to engage the cognitive curiosities of the student in the classroom. Teachers need to become the mentors and facilitators for learning, not the test trainers and givers on an annual multiple-choice test.

We must employ effective school research from true educators to begin on the road to recovery after a decade of decline. Quality instruction from well-versed instructors is the only way to reengage the student in the classroom. We must put "teaching to the test" in the trashcan and restructure our schools to educate our children according to their potentials.

Inclusion students must have all the supports and aids necessary as mandated by IDEA if they are to succeed in the mainstream classroom and not detract from those without special needs. At the same time, the average and above average students should receive the supports and services from their classroom teacher to reach their potential and grow in cognitive ability throughout the school year.

Using current data is important in the restructuring process: the increase in high school dropouts and the percentage of students not college-ready are wake-up calls for policy makers and educators alike. Developing curricula that encourages discovery and problem solving is a must for the twenty-first century. Walk into a classroom where students use authentic learning. Experience and feel the excitement in the air: role-play, debate, Socratic seminar, presentation, experiments, data collection, community involvement. All of these raise the level on engagement, learning, and achievement. We must move away from the drudgery of training to take a test toward an enlightened curriculum that develops interest and perseverance.

TEACHER PREPARATION

The American Association for College Teacher Education sets a guideline for knowledge for twenty-first-century citizenry. It emphasizes the need for basic core academic understanding, explaining the need for basics before moving to higher-level skills. No longer employing people to work in factories on assembly lines, new skills are required to keep pace with rapidly moving technology in every area. Now, more than ever, students need to be flexible in their thinking and able to navigate new information and apply it to current and future contexts.

Teacher colleges and universities need to move out of twentieth-century curricula and update their pedagogical knowledge. Visiting schools and continuing research are the orders for the day. Professors must remove themselves from their comfort levels in the college classroom and immerse themselves into the diversity of needs in the public school. Requirements for a semester teaching in an elementary, middle, or high school every two years just might help advance new levels of instruction for future teachers.

Policy makers and politicians should be supporters, not detractors, for the public school teacher. Instead of bashing and using the failure of our schools as a political platform, they should become familiar with the importance of a good education for all citizens, visit schools in their districts, speak to educators, and help lift the profession to new heights of excellence.

Law makers and advocates for students with special needs need to maintain support for equal opportunity for those with disabilities but also see the importance of maintaining a high level of instruction for all the other students in the classroom. Using a variety of placements to meet the needs for all students is imperative if we are to raise the standard of achievement in our public schools. Full inclusion with the aids and supports for those needing extra help, mainstreaming into classrooms where strengths can be maximized, and special classes for content and integration for extra-curricular are some of the venues possible to maximize achievements and minimize distractions.

STANDARDIZED TESTING

Standardized testing has taken over the public school system. Prior to NCLB, standardized tests measured growth for improvement or mastery. The tests informed teachers and educators, in general, where they might need to focus and when to move on. They were only one measure and could be used as a comparative analysis to other forms of assessment throughout the year.

Teachers and administrators worked collaboratively to seek improvements or enrichments.

Today, the tests threaten funding, teacher jobs, and student advancement. They do not take into account the environment, socioeconomic factors, inclusion students, or multiple learning styles. The once-a-year test has become so onerous, teachers are doing little bedsides preparing for this uninformative piece of paper.

Assessing the effects of the current system of testing has wrought little evidence of growth. We continue to fall behind internationally, we are decreasing the engagement of students in the classroom, and we are no longer attracting high-quality candidates into the field of teaching.

There is no doubt we need to assess our students; we need to see their basic knowledge and then evaluate their ability to think critically, assess, discover, and problem solve. It is time to use various forms of assessment for comparative analysis to measure the learning growth of all students in our care.

Let's rethink, revolutionize, and reform a broken system into a strength for students, schools, and society.

PRINCIPALS

Principals, stay focused on the child—you are their advocate. Preparing administrators with the capacity to improve instruction for all learners is critical and challenging. One of the most important challenges in education is to create and nurture inclusive environments that support learning for all students. The degree to which students can be well educated is directly correlated to a system of personnel preparation that results in a qualified workforce so that every student has highly skilled, competent teachers and administrators. While the law promotes, supports, and protects students with disabilities, little focus and research does the same for general education. In an effort to increase student achievement in classrooms, NCLB requires that highly qualified teachers teach all students.

Every administrator appreciates how teacher quality and quantity directly link to student learning results. The second-most influential factor on student success is the principal and leadership.

QUALIFIED TEACHERS

Hiring and retaining qualified teachers is key. Raising the quality in our schools, states, and districts will strengthen the education profession. Ideally, teachers should have four-year degrees with a major in the subject or subjects they plan to teach. Those who enter teaching should be well educated. They should pass qualifying examinations for entry into professional education programs by demonstrating command of reading, writing, and mathematical skills, as well as mastery of their subject or discipline. Teachers should have mentors. The school and the district should provide frequent opportunities for professional development, collaboration, and intellectual stimulation for teachers, giving them opportunities to learn more about the field as well as to work with colleagues who share their interest. Principals should be chosen from the ranks of master teachers. Before they become principals, they should have at least seven or eight years of experience in the classroom. Their most important job as principal will be to evaluate and help teachers. They can't do that unless they are accomplished teachers themselves, according to Ravitch (2012).

STAFF DEVELOPMENT

When asked what they want for their children, parents and community members overwhelmingly agree that they want the best teacher possible in every classroom. Research confirms that the most important factor contributing to a student's success in school is the quality of teaching. While parents may not be familiar with the research, they are united in their desire to ensure great teaching for every child, every day.

Professional development is the most effective strategy schools and school districts have to meet this expectation. Investment in professional development is the strategy schools and school districts use to ensure that educators continue to strengthen their practice throughout their career. The most effective professional development engages teams of teachers to focus on the needs of their students. They learn and problem solve together in order to ensure all students achieve success. School systems use a variety of schedules to provide this collaborative learning and work time for teachers. When time set aside for professional development is used effectively and parents receive reports about student results, parents realize that the benefits to teachers and their students far outweigh the scheduling inconvenience.

For teachers and school and district leaders to be as effective as possible, they continually expand their knowledge and skills to implement the best educational practices. Educators learn to help students learn at the highest levels.

Many people may not be aware of their local school system's methods for improving teaching and student learning. Professional development is the only strategy school systems have to strengthen educators' performance levels. Professional development is also the only way educators can learn so that they are able to better their performance and raise student achievement.

As in all professions, new teachers and principals take years to gain the skills they need to be effective in their roles. The complexity of teaching is so great that one-third of teachers leave the profession within three years and 50 percent leave within five years (Ingersoll, 2003). Even experienced teachers confront great challenges each year, including changes in subject content, new instructional methods, advances in technology, changes in laws and procedures, and new student learning needs. Educators who do not experience effective professional development do not improve their skills, and student learning suffers.

Most states have laws that require school districts to provide a minimum number of days of professional development, and states provide some funding for this purpose. Canadian provinces also address this requirement. States also may require periodic professional development as a condition for educators to renew their license. Many federal education grant programs provide professional development funding. Federal programs usually include guidelines for state and school district professional development. Some federal agencies also provide direct professional development experiences.

SCHOOLS AS CULTURES OF PROFESSIONAL LEARNING

The powerful collaboration that characterizes professional learning communities is a systematic process in which teachers work together to analyze and improve their classroom practice. Teachers work in teams, engaging in an ongoing cycle of questions that promote deep team learning. This process, in turn, leads to higher levels of student achievement.

What are the benefits of professional learning communities?

Not surprisingly, researchers found that having strong professional learning communities in schools led to many positive cultural changes, including reduced teacher isolation, increased peer learning, increased content knowledge, increased knowledge of effective teaching strategies, greater job satisfaction, and higher teacher retention rates. Researchers also found that the more schools function as professional learning communities, the greater the gains in student learning and improved teacher practice.

An initially low-performing teacher can have a greater positive impact on student achievement when they work in an environment with strong social capital (i.e., where there are opportunities to learn from other knowledgeable colleagues, where there are frequent interactions among colleagues, and where there is a high level of trust).

A recent study (DuFour et al., 2010) both confirms these earlier findings and explores the distinction between the effects of a professional learning community (what the author labels "social capital," measured by surveys of teachers) and the effects of teachers' individual ability (what the author labels "human capital," measured by teachers' education experience in the classroom).

The research findings showed that when the relationships among teachers in a school are characterized by high trust and frequent interaction—that is, when social capital is strong—student achievement scores improve (pp. 23–24). Not only did the students of teachers with both high human capital and social capital have the largest achievement gains and the students of teachers with both low human capital and social capital have the smallest achievement gains, but interestingly "even the low ability teachers can perform as well as teachers of average ability if they have strong social capital" (pp. 38–39). These findings suggest that a strong professional learning community is a powerful strategy for improving teacher effectiveness across the board.

INCLUSIVE COMMUNITIES

Successful promotion and implementation of inclusive education require the five following systems-level practices: (1) connection with other organizational best practices, (2) visionary leadership and administrative support, (3) redefined roles and relationships among adults and students, (4) collaboration, and (5) additional adult support when needed (Villa & Thousand, 2003).

For inclusive education to succeed, administrators must take action to publicly articulate the new vision, build consensus for the vision, and lead all stakeholders to active involvement. Administrators can provide four types of support identified as important by frontline general and special educators: (1) personal and emotional (e.g., being willing to listen to concerns); (2) informational (e.g., providing training and technical assistance); (3) instrumental (e.g., creating time for teachers to meet); and (4) appraisal (e.g., giving constructive feedback related to implementation of new practices) (Littrell, Billingsley, & Cross, 1994).

ACCURATE ASSESSMENTS AND PROGRESS TRACKING

Another important tool for success is the use of informative assessments to build a database tracking each child's growth, development, and progress. In the new world of education, where children of all abilities, backgrounds, languages, and talents are being taught together—often in the same classrooms, by the same teachers—accurate, timely assessments are more important than ever. With universal standards, much testing, and new models for determining how much children have gained (often called "gain scores"), there is a lot of data there for teachers and schools to use. But how? The model we suggest resembles a "systems" model, where schools strive to measure the inputs, throughputs, and outputs, and, over time, see how schools, teachers, and classrooms are operating and producing results (the outputs).

1. *Inputs*—The U.S.A. spends over two trillion dollars on its Pre-K through twelfth grade education, which pays for 3.2 million teachers; 550,000 administrators; and numerous other staff and professionals. We need to track these resources to improve uses of resources and the results of the funding, staffing training, and school programs and activities. And, importantly, we need means to ensure that each student, whatever his or her abilities and needs, is receiving the sufficient and adequate resources in terms of funding, programs, staff, and services.

2. *Throughputs*—How do we determine the most efficient and effective way to run our schools and teach our students? A flexible and appropriate program to help *every* child is critical, since we know that children of different abilities and backgrounds often need different attention and resources to learn in the classroom and in their schools. Thus, assessing and improving teaching practices, programs, and pedagogy in classrooms, labs, and testing center are critical if we are to see real learning and progress.

3. *Outputs*—Perhaps the most important step in assessment is the final one: How are students learning and benefiting from the use of resources and programs? The most recent and controversial measure of outputs are students' gain scores, the value-added model of assessments. What did students know and not know at the start of the year, the programs, the class, and how much did they learn and improve during the time period?

Schools are using gain scores as a way of seeing how well students are doing and how much they learned over a term, semester, or year. The scores determine what the student knew and could do (and tested at what level) at the beginning of the course and what they learned, knew, and tested at the end. Students move at their own speed, learn differently, and have different outcomes. The gain score is critical if we are to track the growth of each student and to determine what he or she learned over a given time period.

Until we can measure the growth and what works to increase learning for each and every child, educators will not know whether teaching practices are effective or not. Lee A. Becker (2013) explains, "The general approach to a gain score analysis is: (a) to compute the gain score, and then (b) analyze those gain scores in an analysis of variance with treatment as the between-subjects factor. This 'output' measure compares each student against his or her former and current knowledge, to see just how much the student learned and thus how well the classroom practices are working" (p. 83).

ADAPTIVE TECHNOLOGIES FOR ALL

Nowhere are poor students—in less well-endowed schools—more likely to be disadvantaged than in uses and advantages of education technology. While few teachers know exactly what technology means and how it helps all students, we do know that the future lies with kids and their schools learning how best to use computers and systems to teach, access information, drill, and thrill children, so they can learn and know the best sources of data, systems, and materials—at all times.

Clearly computers and other technology have serious advantages for those students who have and can access technology inside and outside of their schools. Some of these adaptive technologies are:

1. *Data Access*—Virtually nothing now is not available online, including information materials, books, and ideas. Schools for all children should help their students use computers and other methods for accessing, using, and writing about information. Why memorize when one can access, record, and use?
2. *Writing and Editing*—Virtually anyone who writes or edits today uses a computer, software that helps edit and proof essays, and automated ways of transmitting work to reviewers and publishers, as well as direct avenues to audiences and readers. All children should have an equal chance to learn and practice, write, and calculate online, In fact, with mobile devices, one can exchange ideas from anywhere, anytime, with anyone.
3. *Instant Communications*—No one is alone with technology in hand. Schools and all students—whatever their locations, abilities, background, languages, skill levels—should be given access to others at school, at home, and places in between.
4. *Adapting Curricula and Pedagogy to All Students*—Every school and classroom (and teacher and administrator) could and should be a curriculum writer, adapting what they teach to those they are teaching, in each subject and at each level. Once we retire the old,

dusty, heavy print textbooks and go to online methods, many more children should be accommodated and advance (see Miles & Cooper, 2009).

5. *Building Vocabularies and Test Capacity*—Why not teach vocabulary and word roots on computers, noting that word plurals can be Latin (e.g., alumnus/i, alumna/ae), Greek (hypothesis/es), and even Hebrew (cherub/im, seraph /im, plural of angels)? Or word meanings could be shown, illustrated, and defined (such as mean [nasty], mean [average], mean [definition], mien [facial expression]; or rein, reign, and rain).

6. *Data on Schools, Classrooms, Teachers, and Programs*—Technology may also be used, as it is in many places now, to organize, manage, and report data on schools, teachers, children, programs, and curricula over time.

These examples are but a few. Schools can reach and serve more, if not all children, if technology were available to help monitor, educate, and build skills for the twenty-first century. It's there. It's time—if we can only distribute, train on, and use it.

ENGAGE AND CHALLENGE ALL STUDENTS

The current system of testing has disrupted and disengaged the purpose of public education. Parents, teachers, educational experts, and administrators are bewailing "teaching to the test" and ignoring curricula meant to prepare today's youth to carry us forward in the twenty-first century.

A Nation at Risk, a report published by the National Commission on Excellence in Education in 1983, stirred panic among policy makers and educators, causing a gradual shift toward more and more assessment practices. Today we have structured our whole public education system around tests that have not only disengaged students but have also frustrated even the most professional and qualified educators.

Adding to the stress of testing are policies that mandate including those with special needs in the collective data of school and state-wide assessments. School, teachers, and administrators are all evaluated on the outcomes of yearly tests. The result: teach to the test above everything else and disengage the interest of the average and above average student in the classroom.

The nation is now more at risk than ever before. It is time to revolt, reform, and renew our policies; keep politicians out of the classroom; allow educators to develop sound practices to reignite the excitement learning can bring; and promote the principles of interest exploration, critical thinking, problem solving, and discovery into education.

We need to reimagine schools as institutions that apply the basic principles learned through discovery and application. Begin in the elementary years, eliminating frustrating tests before young minds are ready. Figure 11.1 is taken from a first grader taking a standardized test. He was instructed to select the correct answer, done on a separate sheet, and mark the corresponding number on a Scantron.

As noted in the picture, he simply colored in all items and then cried. There really needs to be no explanation concerning the unjust and unethical treatment of the young mind.

Schools should use informative assessments with the purpose of removing barriers inhibiting understanding and educational growth; teach (and reteach) basics necessary to develop opportunity for more challenging tasks; and challenge students with authentic-based learning. What better way to learn than to apply higher-order thinking skills to find an answer to a question or a solution to a problem.

Case in point: The chicken and cow problem, traditionally an algebraic problem, was observed in a second-grade classroom. The teacher presented the dilemma in a story to her class and asked if the students would help this poor farmer figure out how many cows and chickens he had.

The teacher presented materials for use but gave no directions or procedures. The students worked in pairs or triads, first discussing the process they would use (drawing pictures, stick figures, using numbers, etc.),

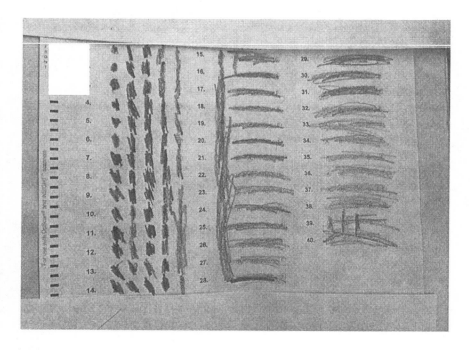

Figure 11.1.   1st Grade Scan-Sheet by a Child — "Fast" Answers from Little Kids

and proceeded to solve a problem usually given to middle school students. The depth of discussion and the excitement of discovery were electrifying for all, and when the problem was solved, the teacher had each group relate their method of solution. There were no algebraic formulas but lots of drawings of heads, legs, and stick figures. (Observation of a 2nd grade teacher by author, J. Mulvey.)

Learning isn't just rote memorization for a test but an excitement, according to Muir (2001): "When you realize that people learn naturally from the life they experience—the brain is set up to learn better with active hands-on endeavors" (p. 39).

By making real-world connections, creating schools that are inviting instead of threatening, reapplying Bloom's Taxonomy for learning, removing barriers for failure, encouraging discovery, and celebrating multiple ways of learning, we can assess real outcomes for real, everyday problem solving and critical thinking.

RESEARCH THE CONDITIONS THAT BOTH HAMPER AND IMPROVE COGNITIVE AND SOCIAL DEVELOPMENT

Research on developmental milestones, multiple intelligences, cognitive theory, diverse learning styles, environmental influences, and socioeconomic conditions are rich and complex when discussing conditions that encourage and/or hamper learning among young children and older students in our public schools.

A Nation at Risk (National Commission on Excellence in Education, 1983) caused grave concerns about the education of our children in the United States. Thirty years have passed, and the United States continues to push reform movements forward with little or no results. As a matter of fact, the most recent report concerning our international standing indicates that we have declined, placing us thirty-first in mathematics and stagnant in other tested areas (Walker, 2013). Whereas other nations continue to improve, we are worsening. According to Graham (2013), "Some problems that *A Nation at Risk* raised three decades ago have been made worse in the face of budget cuts and other reforms" (np).

The United States continues to push reforms created by corporations and publishing magnates who profit from our failures. And as NEA President Dennis Van Roekel cites, "Educators across the country work hard to give their students the education they deserve, but lawmakers cannot keep pulling the rug out from under them with bad ideas" (quoted in Graham, 2013, np).

Teaching should not be based on ideas formulated by policy makers, politicians, and lobbying corporations but on sound educational and research-founded principles. We have learned over the years that unlike Dewey claims that young children are empty vessels ready to be filled, eager to learn by hands-on exploration and discovery. So how do we construct learning in the twenty-first-century technology-based world?

What do the top countries do to engage, excite, and achieve?

What strategies do we implement to turn our "teach to the test" mentality to the world of learning?

1. Invest in education in the United States. Increase commitment to improve the physical conditions of our classroom and schools, provide resources for twenty-first-century learning. Create standard class sizes, regardless of socioeconomic environments.
2. Attract teachers through positive support and fair pay. Finland pays all teachers the same according to their experience, not their location. Respect the profession and remove political criticisms.
3. Provide early preschool, especially for immigrant, ESL, and impoverished children to develop the basic language and verbal ability to enter public school ready to learn. Sampson (2007) explains, "Children living in disadvantaged neighborhoods appears to contribute to a detrimental effect on trajectories of verbal ability" (np).
4. Alter lecture/rote information input to cooperative, interactive, hands-on, engaging assignments. Young minds flourish with strategies that make them think and solve, not remember and regurgitate.
5. Model metacognitive thinking in the classroom to help students develop their own strategies for problem solving and creative thinking.
6. Apply content to context, whether in the classroom, the community, or their lives, to excite and make learning meaningful.
7. Respect the potential for other talents that may or may not be academic in nature but vocational.
8. Research the methodologies of countries with the highest success rates and configure them to our own demographic society.

Children are our greatest resource for the future. As a country we need to support that resource with proven methodology not profit or political motivations.

FINANCING FOR AN EFFECTIVE EDUCATION FOR ALL STUDENTS

Recommendations for better school funding are complex but possible. First, we have to understand the governance levels: no, not three (federal, state, local) but five levels, including school and classroom. Somehow we must drive dollars to the child in the school and classroom to see that resources reach the children where they need funding, programs, and help.

Second, we need to push for equity at the school and classroom levels so that funds are reaching the students and not lost in the bureaucracies. We were hired by New York City Mayor Rudy Giuliani in 1985 to design a method for determining the "functions" that dollars paid for (e.g., administration, buildings, support, and classroom instruction). We found that only about 30 percent reached the classroom (to pay teachers and purchase direct materials, books, and equipment for instruction). After the city implemented our model, called In$ite™, or the Finance Analysis Model (FAM), the amount reaching the school rose, and the percentage in classroom for direct, face-to-face instruction had reached 65 percent.

Finally, the needs and requirements of children—whether gifted, at the mean, or below average or disabled—must be part of the funding formula, so children who need help or need greater challenges get them.

SUPPORTS AND SERVICES FOR INCLUSION

In the inclusive setting, students with special needs and general education students work side by side in the same classroom. One concern is that the general education teacher may not have had training in working with special education students. It is imperative that the teacher in the inclusive classroom has support from the special education teacher, paraprofessionals, and related service providers. The special education teacher will be able to support the general education teacher in differentiating the curriculum to meet the needs of all students, promote positive interdependence among students in the class, as well as ensure that the classroom teacher is able to fulfill the goals on the special education student's IEP.

Support may also come from the many related service providers and paraprofessionals in the building. They are able to support all students in their classroom setting in areas ranging from the speech therapist helping students with communication skills to the occupational therapists working on fine motor skills with students to the school psychologist or social worker supporting students with social or behavioral issues and developing behavior plans for those students who need them.

Greater inclusion of students with diverse needs into general education classes and other integrated environments has created the need for support personnel to modify their traditional methods of service provision. Specifically, structures that allow support personnel to observe and work with students and their teachers and peers in the context of their educational programs are essential to ensure the educational relevance of their support. This requires two major logistical changes: (1) flexible scheduling so that support personnel can spend time in general education classes and other integrated environments and (2) scheduling opportunities for the people involved to collaborate (York, Giangreco, Vander-cook, and Macdonald, 1992, cited in Stainback & Stainback, 1992) .

Support may look different in each school, what is important is that the support being offered provides the classroom teacher with opportunities for in-service training, peer coaching, professional development, and opportunities for collaborative consultations, all in the interest of meeting the diverse needs of all students.

SMALLER CLASSES WITH MORE RESOURCES

Teachers involved in coteaching suggest that having a supportive administrator, such as the school principal, is essential to success. The principal can ensure that they have the resources needed, such as time to plan and collaborate, and professional development.

Teachers reported receiving very little training to prepare them for c-teaching as one of the main obstacles to forming a successful coteach setting. Many of them would have liked training in collaboration, co-teaching models, communication skills, and inclusive practices to help them work together and in each other's areas of expertise (e.g., content-area instruction for special educators and information on various disabilities for general educators) (Scruggs, Mastropieri, & McDuffie, 2007).

Coteaching teams need to work together effectively in order to provide the students with a classroom that works for them. This means there needs to be clear expectations set from the beginning, with both teachers sharing an equal role in the instruction of the students. Unfortunately some districts implement coteaching to meet their needs, not the needs of the students. Having a special education teacher in the classroom for only part of the day or as a consultant does not follow the true model of coteaching. One of the benefits of coteaching is that there are two educators in the classroom at all times, addressing the needs of the students. While they may not teach at the same time, they are both there to help all students. Often one teacher is teaching while the other is free to circulate the classroom, working with students who need more support. This method is believed to increase the effectiveness of coteaching and allows the teachers to focus on student learning outcomes.

In the coteaching model, the class size is not increased because there are two teachers in the classroom, rather it is the same as the general education class sizes or smaller when possible. When putting a coteach class together, schools must keep in mind that the number of students with disabilities in a general education classroom should not exceed 33 percent of the total number of students in that class. Of course, this is just a guideline; the number of students included in the class may be less depending on the situation. Again, this allows for maximum support for all students in the class.

PUSH-IN SERVICES FOR PHYSICAL AND SOCIAL NEEDS

Coteaching affords students with special needs the chance to learn in a classroom with general education students. Many times special education students require the services of support staff such as the speech therapist, social worker, occupational therapist, and physical therapist. It is often the case that when the students receive these services they are removed or "pulled" from the classroom. A better alternative would be to have the service providers "push" into the classroom and provide the services in the classroom. When the students are pulled from the classroom, they miss the academics that are being delivered while they are out of the room as well as the social interactions. While most teachers do find time in the day to reteach the lesson to those students who missed it because of pull-outs, it is not the same as when delivered to the entire class. They miss the class discussion and interaction between peers, which can be just as valuable as the lesson itself.

Push-in services are also known as integrated classroom-based or classroom-based services. The belief is that providing the services in the classroom has a positive impact on the student's academic performance. The service provider works with the classroom teachers to determine the skills or strategies that will be worked on. These lessons benefit all students in the coteach classroom. The service provider may work with small groups of students or the entire class.

These lessons are woven into the classroom curriculum, in hopes that they will be carried over into other areas of the student's day.

AFFECTING CHANGE THROUGH LEADERSHIP

School leaders know to affect change takes not only a vision but also the ability to get all the stakeholders to share that vision. A district looking to implement inclusive classrooms as part of its repertoire of best practices in education may need to educate teachers, administrators, parents, and community members. As with any change, there needs to be a clear plan set in place, with one leader directing the change. Looking at districts with similar demographics, who have successfully implemented inclusion may be helpful. They are better able to tell you what worked well for them and what didn't work as they implemented the plan. Spending time visiting the school and observing the classrooms will give teachers and administrators an idea of what inclusion looks like once it's up and running. Looking at their timeline and budget will also be helpful in guiding districts that are just starting on their own implementation plan.

As educational leaders continue to struggle with the "highly qualified teacher" mandate of the No Child Left Behind (NCLB) legislation, many are turning to coteaching models that are designed to incorporate regular education and special education teachers into the same classroom to deliver instruction. This model appears to address the issue of inclusion of students with disabilities into the regular classroom while simultaneously eliminating the NCLB mandate that all teachers must be highly qualified in the subjects in which they instruct (Nicholas, Dowdy, Nicholas, 2010).

A coteaching situation allows general education teachers and special education teachers to form an educational partnership for the purpose of delivering high-quality education to diverse populations. It is a way of ensuring that students with special needs have access to the same opportunities and curriculum as general education students. It is believed that students with disabilities, average students, and gifted students benefit from this option when it is implemented properly.

COLLABORATION

Teachers are on the front line of this initiative. They will need appropriate professional development from a qualified staff developer, including in-service classes, mentoring, coteaching, and support from the coaches, if available. General education and special education teachers will need time to collaborate. There also needs to be time for collaboration between the teachers and the support staff in the building, as their roles are about to change as well. Each being an expert in their field, they have much to share and teach the other. Hopefully this will be the beginning of a true collaboration that lasts many years. Time must be allotted for this collaboration during the school day; the teachers and support staff should not be expected to do this on their time. As with anything new and different, the more support that is offered, the more willing the participants will be to implement the change.

Reports from school districts throughout the United States identify collaboration as a key variable in the successful implementation of inclusive education. Creating planning teams, scheduling time for teachers to work and teach together, recognizing teachers as problem solvers, conceptualizing teachers as frontline researchers, and effectively collaborating with parents are all dimensions reported as crucial to successful collaboration (National Center on Educational Restructuring and Inclusion, 1995).

There also needs to be planning teams set in place that will deal with the day-to-day logistics that arise as the school moves through the changes. As with anything else, issues will arise that could not have been foreseen. Having a team available to handle these issues and get answers to the parties involved eliminates stress and confusion before it can start.

Even the best of plans can go astray when roles are subject to change. Inclusive classrooms change the roles of the teacher and students; even a change for the better is difficult without the right direction and support from administrators. General education teachers need training in their legal responsibilities for meeting the goals on a student's individualized education plan (IEP). Administrators need to be certain that teachers know how to differentiate the instruction in the classroom to meet the needs of all learners.

Lastly, school leaders need to recognize that teachers are problem solvers—that is what they do in the classroom all day long, whether it's a problem between two students or how to help a student understand a difficult concept. Teachers may be able to work through some of the problems that may come up during this time of change. Having the teachers involved as much as possible in the planning and implementation of inclusion can only help. Inclusion is a big change for them as well. Classroom teachers know the importance of home and school working together for the benefit of the student. Who better to talk to the parents and answer their questions than the teacher who will be implementing the change in the school?

Change takes time. In order to have a successful transformation, schools should think about implementing inclusion on a small scale and then adding to it each year. An example might be to start in two grades, add two more the following years, and so on. This gives the district time to oversee the project closely, work out any issues that arise and educate all the necessary parties involved in the process. Implemented properly, with appropriate supports, small class size, and expertise from both general education and special education teachers, coteaching may benefit all students involved and provide a much-needed solution to the conundrum of educational inclusion.

REFERENCES

Becker, L. A. (2013). *Effect size calculations*. Colorado Springs: University of Colorado.

DuFour, R., DuFour, R., Eaker, R., & Many, T. (2010). *Learning by doing: A handbook for professional communities at work, 2nd edition*. Bloomington, IN: Solution Tree Press.

Fisher, D., & Frey, N. (2001). Access to the core curriculum: Critical ingredients for student success. *Remedial and Special Education, 22*(3), 148–157.

Graham, E. (2013, April 25). "A Nation at Risk" turns 30: Where did it take us? *neatoday.org*. Retrieved from http://neatoday.org/2013/04/25/a-nation-at-risk-turns-30-where-did-it-take-us/.

Ingersoll, R. (2003). *Who controls teachers' work? Power and accountability in America's schools*. Cambridge, MA: Harvard University Press.

Littrell, P. C., Billingsley, B. S., & Cross, L. H. (1994). The effects of principal support on special and general educators' stress, job satisfaction, school commitment, health, and intent to stay in teaching. *Remedial and Special Education, 15*, 297–310.

Miles, M., & Cooper, B. S. (2009). Reimagining the textbook: The risks and reward of electronic reading devices. *Education Week, Commentary, 11*(November 11), 54–55.

Muir, M. (2001). What engages underachieving middle school students in learning? *Middle School Journal, 33*(2), 37–43.

National Center on Educational Restructuring and Inclusion. (1995). *National study on inclusive education.* New York: City University of New York.

National Commission on Excellence in Education. (1983). *A nation at risk: The imperative for educational reform.* Washington, DC: U.S. Department of Education.

Nicholas, J., Dowdy, A., Nicholas, C. (2010). Co-teaching: An educational promise for children with disabilities or a quick fix to meet the mandates of no child left behind? *Education, 130,* 647–651.

Ravitch, D. (2012). A Chicago teacher: Why I am striking. *Ravitch Blog.* September 12, 2012.

Sampson, R. (2007). In: *Living in a disadvantaged neighborhood is equivalent to missing a year in school.* http://news.harvard.edu/gazette/story/2007/12/living-in-disadvantaged-neighborhood-equivalent-to-missing-a-year-of-school/.

Scruggs, T. E., Mastropieri, M. A., & McDuffie, K. A. (2007). Co-teaching in inclusive class-rooms: A metasynthesis of qualitative research. *Exceptional Children, 73*(4), 392–416.

Stainback, S., & Stainback, W. (1992). *Curriculum considerations in inclusive classrooms: Facilitating learning for all students.* Baltimore: Paul H. Brookes.

Villa, R. A., & Thousand, J. S. (2003). Making inclusive education work. *Educational Leadership, 61*(2), 19–21.

Walker, T. (2013). "A nation at risk" turns 30: Where did it take us? http://neatoday.org/2013/04/25/a-nation-at-risk-turns-30-where-did-it-take-us/.

Index

test motivation, 120
tracking, 93
traditional students. *See* students,
  general education
training, 121

United States (U.S.): college readiness
  in, 13–14; colleges and students
  from, ix; demographic changes in,
60–62; education impact on, viii–ix,
22, 34, 108; inclusion and
international standing of, 8–9, 141;
teacher training impact on, 53
universal design for learning, 80
U.S. *See* United States

wealth, 10–11, 56
work quantity, 94–95

CPSIA information can be obtained at www.ICGtesting.com
Printed in the USA
BVOW07s1929300614

357802BV00002B/6/P